The
SeaLand Incident

The Story Behind One Zoo's Infamous Attempt to House a Great White Shark

Brent Saltzman

Text copyright © 2016 by Brent Saltzman

THE SEALAND INCIDENT

All rights reserved.

ISBN-13: 978-0692826355
ISBN-10: 0692826351

10 9 8 5 7 6 3 2 1 05 06 07 08 09

Printed in the U.S.A.
First American Edition: November 2016

To Carson and Bentley. May you both one day love sharks as much as I.

1

It All Made Sense at the Time

I t all seemed rather simple, to be honest." Those were the first words from Dr. Anna Harding after I'd asked her just what the staff of SeaLand was thinking during those few notorious months over the summer of 2015. A moment before, I'd flipped on my recorder and sat back to enjoy the warm breeze of South Carolina's early spring. A daiquiri sweated on the table in front of me and the Atlantic Ocean stretched out over the globe behind me. Waves softly broke over white sands and the few patrons of the beachfront restaurant that early afternoon kept their chatter to a minimum.

"Simple?" I asked, raising an eyebrow. "It's one of the most dangerous animals in the world. The word 'simple' doesn't exactly come to mind when I think of it."

Dr. Harding laughed as if she'd been expecting such a reply. I got the sense she'd heard it many times. Hundreds, even, especially over the court proceedings some months prior. She went on to explain that zoos and aquariums actually had a lot of success with giant predators. In fact, an enormous saltwater crocodile was being kept not five miles away, at Myrtle Beach's famous Alligator Adventure—the closest thing you'll find to a real life Jurassic Park in the

The SeaLand Incident

United States.

Saltwater crocodiles, *Crocodylus porosus,* are the largest reptiles on the planet. Topping out at over 20 feet, these gigantic animals easily reach 3,000 pounds and are among the animal kingdom's deadliest apex predators. Their diets consist mostly of large mammals, but they've been known to eat sharks, other crocodiles, and the occasional human.

Lying in the shallows, these monstrous animals wait for passing prey before launching themselves from the water, crunching down with enough bite force to snap bones. If you're looking for the closest living equivalent to what we imagine as dinosaurs, the saltwater crocodile is your best bet.

An obscure story from World War II involves an attack on Japanese soldiers by saltwater crocodiles. The story goes that several hundred soldiers—though exact numbers are difficult to come by—attempted to cross the inland mangrove swamps near Ramree Island in order launch a sneak attack on some British troops. However, by morning only a few dozen Japanese soldiers remained, the rest purportedly eaten by the massive saltwater crocodiles that inhabited those muddy waters.

The Guinness World Records named the Ramree Island incident as the single most devastating mass animal attack in human history, but its validity remains questionable. Some argue that the numbers have been inflated over time, and that actual history had been diluted by sensationalism. This is probably true. Regardless, there have been plenty of documented attacks on humans by not only saltwater crocodiles, but their slightly smaller cousins, the Nile crocodiles, *Crocodylus niloticus.*

Since the year 2000 alone, dozens of people had been killed and eaten by crocodiles. Gustave, a large Nile crocodile given the moniker the "Beast of Burundi," is so notorious that a feature film based off its purportedly hundreds of kills was made in 2007. The animal has never been captured and its reputation has grown from pesky nuisance to murderous serial killer. In 2005, a man was eaten by a saltwater crocodile while snorkeling off Picnic Beach. In 2009, a small child was killed by one in northern Australia. In 2010, a 25-year-old woman was viciously attacked in India (while her boyfriend filmed the event). The list goes on and on...

Which brings us to Utan.

By now, it's more than obvious that the saltwater crocodile is no less than a living dinosaur, a relic of the time of monsters, and lives up to its fierce reputation with overwhelming veracity. They are gigantic, aggressive, hyper-carnivorous apex predators and the well-established kings of the terrestrial food chain.

Yet, to an extent, we have managed to domesticate them.

I visited the Alligator Adventure during my time in Myrtle Beach. It's a bit off the beaten path, several miles from the hotels and street vendors of the boardwalk. I conducted no interviews during my visit; I was just another tourist, paying my seventeen-dollar admission fee and wandering around the relatively small open park.

The park consists of many interconnecting wooden pathways, all surrounding different pools that served as enclosures for various crocodilians. There was a small building with snake cages and a stage somewhere in the middle where a young woman held baby alligators in front of smiling children.

More than a few pools had standard American alligators, *Alligitor mississippiensis,* a common sight on golf courses through the southeastern United States. They were smaller in person than most people probably visualized, topping out at around five to six feet, with some rare specimens attaining approximately double that length in the wild. They were also quite boring. I stood over the fence, looking down into the pools for some time and very rarely did I see any actual movement. The animals were content to just bask in the sun and stare at the visitors pointing down into their enclosures, bemoaning their lack of activity.

I will admit that it was frustrating to watch fish literally swim right up to an alligator's nose, pick at it, then swim away unharmed. I wanted to see these fierce reptiles in action. I wanted to see that prehistoric ferocity that movies and TV shows had promised. I wanted to see this reptile's primordial bloodlust and capture it squarely within the sensor of my small digital camera so I could post it on social media and get a like or two. But the alligator had no interest in satisfying my craving.

Luckily, Utan did.

Utan's enclosure was significantly larger than every other cage in the park, and unlike the other inhabitants, he had it to himself. It consisted of a grassy plain that descended into a sandy beach and eventually an underground pool of murky water. Unlike the other enclosures, which had only rudimentary, waist-high railings, Utan's pen was surrounded by a 20-foot-tall wall of meshed steel more appropriate for Velociraptors than the relatively puny alligators I'd been snapping photos of all day.

I joined the crowd of onlookers and squinted through the wire mesh. Utan was in the pool at the time, so only his back, eyes, and nostrils were exposed. His massiveness cannot be understated; go ahead and measure out twenty feet. Now imagine a gigantic animal that long, staring you down, with jaws that could tear you apart at a moment's notice. The osteoderms along his back looked like armor plates. The eyes were cold, reptilian. The nostrils flared ever so slightly.

Still, I did not appreciate the majesty of this animal until it emerged from the water.

A number of trainers entered through the grassy side of the enclosure, sporting white shorts, sunglasses and polos. They held hunks of raw chicken out on metal poles. Personally, I would've made the poles a bit longer. And probably been behind the wire mesh. While wearing a suit of armor. Alas, these brave souls approached Utan's pool with a type of relaxed confidence I imagine only could be attained through years of unfulfilled death wishes or psychoactive drugs.

Utan moved toward the pebbly bank of his pool and emerged from the water, the behemoth lumbering toward the park trainers with steady determination. Water dripped from its armored body and its claws dug into the earth with each step. This was a walking tank. I could see bits of flesh still stuck between its teeth from what I presumed were earlier meals. I hoped it was chicken flesh and not that of some poor trainer.

The crowd applauded as one trainer raised the pole, lifting the chicken into the air. Utan complied like a trained dog, raising his head and slowly opening his jaws. The trainer was smiling. Here he was, laughing about serving an obedient dragon lunch.

Utan ripped off the chunk of meat and began snapping his jaws open and shut in a sort of pseudo-chewing motion. Crocodilians don't have the ability to chew properly, so ripping meat apart with their claws or thrashing it about until it tears into swallowable chunks are the best they can do.

When the feeding was over, Utan slunk back into his pool, the plated tail vanishing below the surface while tourists flocked to an underwater viewing window.

I was taken aback by the experience. Not only was Utan an enormous creature, but the indifference it showed toward the trainers was astonishing. Was this an intelligent animal? Did it realize that eating a trainer probably wasn't the best way to ensure a steady supply of Perdue? Was it simply so used to its routine that it was no longer a truly sentient being, only an organic machine that went about its day with all the spontaneity of a mailman on his daily route?

Alligator Adventure had done something I thought impossible. They had taken one of the planet's most vicious and feared creatures and turned it into an exhibit for children. They'd ripped out its teeth (metaphorically), dressed it up, and marched it out at the Westminster Reptile Show.

So it was possible, after all.

An apex carnivore could be captured and made into an attraction.

So, naturally, since the king of the swamps had been dominated by man, the next challenge was the king of the seas: the Great White shark.

Made famous by Peter Benchley's novel *Jaws*—and arguably more so by the 1975 film—the Great White shark, *Carcharodon carcharias*, is the *Tyrannosaurus rex* of the ocean. These massive animals can reach a mature size of 21 feet and weigh three times as much as a saltwater crocodile. There have even been published reports of specimens reaching over 26 feet. To put that in perspective, the titular giant shark in *Jaws* was 25 feet, meaning that the real animals can actually be *bigger* than the fictionalized one.

Those are absolute maximum sizes, of course. The average size of a Great White shark is something around 17 feet, which is still more than twice the length of the average human. Their length is not to be outdone by their robust girth and enormous jaws, which are capable of biting many marine mammals in half.

With its dark gray top and white belly, the beast swims silently through all corners of the globe. Where there's saltwater, there are Great White sharks. They're an iconic species, tingling the spines of surfers and swimmers around the world. A single sighting of their distinct dorsal fins breaking the surface of the water can empty a beach for days. Divers can only encounter them using military-grade cages that still offer scant protection from these solitary leviathans of the deep.

In 2008, a study was conducted by scientist Stephen Wroe to determine the exact bite force of an average Great White. His team used computer models to create a replica of the shark's musculature and jaws, then put it to the test. They concluded that a large specimen could bite with the force of approximately 18,000 newtons. (Also known as *"a lot."*) For comparison's sake, the famed *Tyrannosaurus rex*, a creature nearly three times as long and three times the weight, bit with a force of around 35,000 newtons while modern saltwater crocodiles bite with a force of around 16,000 newtons.

Though, believe me, 18,000 is plenty.

It only takes around 800 newtons for you to bite into your well done steak, not that any stable person would order a wonderful cut of meat in such fashion (I presume).

However, the Great White shark cannot be truly appreciated until it is seen in action, in person, for it has one trait we'd normally not associate with its image: *speed*.

Most clips of the Great White are of it gradually gliding along the open ocean, obscured by haze, but a smooth silhouette in the distance. In these moments, it appears as a slow, dumb giant. But that image is completely false.

Shortly before travelling to Myrtle Beach to interview with Anna Harding, I wanted to see these animals in their natural habitat. I traveled to Cape Town in South Africa, a picturesque little city that matched absolutely no westerner's image of the continent. There were no expansive jungles or lion-filled savannahs here. Cape Town felt more like a city in modern California, with palm trees, pastel-colored buildings, and a surprisingly tolerable climate.

I didn't have time to enjoy the city much, as I was busy participating in a tour of the coastal waters, packed into a small fishing boat with a dozen or so other tourists while a guide pointed out various boring rock formations on the coastline which you couldn't have paid me to show any interest in. After an hour or so of struggling to keep myself awake, we came to the featured event: the Great White shark feeding grounds.

Now, Great Whites are, as stated earlier, solitary animals. They don't make friends. But where there's food to be had, they'll make their way.

We were a few hundred yards off the rocky coastline and the water was teeming with seals. They looked for all the world like puppies with fins instead of feet. They'd frequently approach the boat and rub the hull with their snouts. These animals seemed harmless, friendly, and cute.

So it was a shame that I knew what was going to happen to them.

Like an explosion, a Great White shark leapt from the water, arcing like a diver from a platform, before falling back in with a smack, leaving a bubbling cloud of sea foam while seals scattered in terror. A few seconds later, another shark emerged, leaping into the air and flailing about, the image of a seal struggling in its jaws etched in my mind permanently.

This happened several more times before the seas finally calmed. It was breathtaking seeing animals of such size becoming airborne. There was absolutely nothing to stop them from leaping into the boat, if they so chose, and giving us the same treatment that Jaws gave Quint.

The guide, a small dark-skinned man with long hair and sunglasses, explained in a thick South African accent that the Great White sharks could reach speeds of up to 35 miles per hour. *35 miles per hour!* The average adult swimmer can reach two miles per hour. *Two.* The sharks would dive deep, maneuver their bodies upward, then rocket to the surface with a burst of speed reserved only for the fastest terrestrial animals, chomping an unsuspecting seal on its way up before soaring through the air and landing back into the ocean with a meal.

The aerial ballet was quick and savage. It was clear within moments: these were *deadly* animals. I'd never seen such a rare combination of size, speed, and ferocity. Thank goodness they didn't live on land.

The Great White shark is responsible for the most attacks on humans of any shark worldwide. I asked the guide about the common notion that sharks didn't actually mean to attack humans and simply mistook us for their more common prey items, notably seals, and that they weren't actually as dangerous as they looked. Besides, statistics will tell you that lightning strikes, dogs, or even falling vending machines kill more people every year than Great White sharks.

The guide laughed at me.

Sharks, as he bluntly pointed out, were not the most intelligent creatures on the planet. They ran off instinct. There was no empathy in their eyes, and they didn't leave humans alone after attacking them out of the goodness of their hearts.

Most fatal shark attack victims are never eaten. The shark simply takes a bite then swims away, once realizing that it was a human and not a tasty seal. The reason, my guide (who I assume did not have any sort of degree on the subject, but I'll take his word for it) assured me, was because humans are simply not very good food. Though the western world and its obsession with excess food (myself included) may soon end this trend, the modern human's bone-to-blubber ratio isn't ideal for the shark's diet. They require lots of fat to burn up as a fuel source in order to keep their massive bodies propelling through the water, something (most) humans just can't provide at the same level as seals or other marine mammals.

Then there are the aforementioned statistics. Here is a list of things, in no particular order, that kill more people every year than shark attacks: falling out of beds, choking while trying to blow up a balloon, being crushed by collapsing vending machines, drowning in bathtubs, falling down staircases, being attacked by cows or horses, falling off ladders or even being knocked out by a fallen TV set. These are all things that many bloggers and clickbait writers use to invalidate the danger that sharks present.

And they are all absolutely wrong.

While statistically true that autoerotic asphyxiation kills more people every year than sharks, all of those bloggers tend to ignore one simple fact: *we don't share a habitat with sharks*. We're a terrestrial species that's in constant contact with beds, ladders, bathtubs and odd sexual fantasies. Our interaction with sharks is kept to a minimum, which more than accounts for the low fatality numbers. How many times have you been to the beach and actually encountered a shark? (Though keep in mind, more sharks have seen you than you have seen of them.)

Before I finished my conversation with the guide, he instilled upon me this: these are exceptionally dangerous animals. If you encounter one, and it decides to take your life, there is very little you can do about it. They *should* be both feared and respected as such. They are living monsters, the rulers of the aquatic domain trumped by few other creatures on the earth.

Which brings us back to the first question I had for Dr. Harding that day in April 2016, while having drinks on the pier: "Why did you think this was a good idea?"

She shrugged and smirked, "It all made sense at the time. The park was struggling and the storm trapped it. It was just too good of an opportunity to pass up, both scientifically and from a financial standpoint. And to be fair, it's not like we didn't—or weren't going to, anyway—succeed at what we originally set out to do."

"At the time?" I asked, sipping my terrible fruity drink. I was typically a bourbon man, myself, a taste I had developed in college when feigning an overabundance of masculinity for the bevy of attractive women I was always too terrified to talk to.

"Hindsight's twenty-twenty, right?" she replied.

"Let's go back to that time," I said, "if you don't mind."

The time in question was May 2015, immediately after Tropical Storm Ana ravaged Myrtle Beach. It was during this time that the tiny marine zoological park known as SeaLand would attempt something that had never been done before: the successful capture and permanent housing of the ocean's most revered apex predator.

2
A Brief History of Zoos

The argument that zoos and aquariums are simply an extension of mankind's hubris and our obsession with both containing and controlling the world around us is not a new one. Nor will it be discussed within the confines of this piece. The morality of these institutions is not a debate for this work, nor one I'd dive into even in most other circumstances. Politics are better left to activists and people pretending to be activists on social media.

However, to better understand the thought process of the SeaLand executives and researchers that led to the park's ill-famed incident, it is important to comprehend the history and importance of modern zoological parks and aquariums.

Before zoos were called "zoos," they were "menageries," the oldest of which have been documented going as far back as 3500 BC in, of course, Egypt. Most of the animals kept in menageries were species indigenous to Africa, such as elephants, hippos and various big cats. These specimens were kept not for public display, but as part of a private collection, or as a hobby by those rich enough to afford such luxuries. King Solomon was also a well known collector of animals, and even Alexander the Great was known for sending creatures back to Greece.

One of the more famed early menageries was founded in the mid 1200s within the Tower of London. The Royal Menagerie, as it was called, contained numerous wings specified to different animals, including lions and elephants. This royal collection of animals had become so popular that it was often gifted creatures from around the world, and stood for over 600 years. By the 1700s, the Royal Menagerie contained nearly 300 animals and was even open to the public. The admission price? Either three half-pence or a cat to feed to the lions.

Take your pick.

Sadly (though I imagine to the great relief the city's stray cats), the menagerie was closed in 1835 when a lion bit a soldier. Today, visitors can see wire sculptures of the park's lions standing in its ruins.

The word "zoo" didn't come into popular use until the mid-1800s, used in reference to the Bristol Zoo. The term became popular and was adopted by the London Zoo, which was originally called the Gardens and Menagerie of the Zoological Society of London. The London Zoo opened in 1828, though not to the public until 1847. The world's oldest functioning zoo, the Vienna Zoo, opened in 1752 as an imperial menagerie by the order of the Holy Roman Emperor Francis I. Its original purpose was to entertain members of the royal family, but was eventually made public a decade or so later.

The purpose of the zoo evolved over time from private menagerie for entertainment purposes, to a collection for research purposes, to a little bit of both as it is today. They were originally meant to serve as a symbol of royal power, a poetic statement by a regal figure announcing their control over Mother Nature.

It wasn't until the 19th century that they were established for educational and entertainment purposes. London was a growing city, and the desire to satisfy both a supply of entertainment options and a research institution led to the Zoological Society of London's founding of the London Zoo. While not as old as Vienna's zoo, it is considered the world's first zoo built exclusively for scientific study and public entertainment. Everything about the zoo was designed to cater to London's ever-expanding cityscape, including its open layout that made it accessible from the center of a large urban landscape.

While the London Zoo can be credited as the first scientific zoo, it wasn't until 1907 that the world saw something akin to what we'd expect to see today. Carl Hagenbeck, a German entrepreneur, founded Tierpark Hagenbeck in Hamburg, a zoological park which still stands today. Hagenbeck's zoo used vast open enclosures and moats that simulated the animals' native environments, unlike the simple cages used by the London Zoo at the time. This development proved revolutionary and would be the model that most zoos would use from then to modernity.

By the 1970s, zoos could be found in almost every major city on the planet. However, they were continually forced to shift their focus, and thus their justification for existing, as viewpoints and paradigms evolved. Many zoos now highlight ecological awareness and conservation as their primary goal, and frequently contribute hefty sums of money each year to said causes. In an effort to solidify their stance, many zoos even ceased their popular animal shows, bowing to public thought that the trainers more than likely had to abuse the animals in order to get them to perform properly.

Zoos are constantly evolving their ideals in order to fit modern times and stay relevant, a task that has become particularly difficult in the wake of the "outrage culture" that has plagued the beginning of this millennium. The general public constantly looks for reasons to be angry—often focusing on minutiae and confirmation bias to justify their protests. As a result, zoos have had to conform in order to stay ahead, whether it be by ending breeding programs, giving even more money to conservation groups, or even changing their names. (The National Zoo in Washington DC flirted with calling itself a "biopark" in the late 1980s and the New York Zoological Society changed its name to the Wildlife Conservation Society).

But how do zoos work, exactly? While the answer seems rather simple—put some animals in cages then charge people to look at them—the logistics of building and maintaining a zoo are far more complex than they appear on the surface.

First, there is the legal red tape. In the western world, where there is undoubtedly much more pressure from conservation groups, zoos are strictly regulated. In the United States, a license must first be acquired by the US Department of Agriculture, which involves presenting all plans to the organization and justification of the zoo's existence. This is an enormous task in itself. Everything must be accounted for; the contracting teams building the zoo, the wildlife experts you've pre-hired as consultants, the veterinarians, the facilities you're planning to build, *everything*. And when you do get your license and build your park after years and years of construction, it must be inspected.

The inspections are done by a number of organizations. These include, but are not limited to, the Environmental Protection Agency, the Occupational Safety and Health Administration, and even the Drug Enforcement Administration. (Zoos use a variety of tranquilizers and other chemicals that aren't exactly found at CVS.)

And good luck if you intend on keeping endangered animals, which are incidentally the only kind of animals most people are interested in seeing. There is a whole other slew of laws in regards to the Endangered Species Act that a zoo must comply with in order to even consider displaying something even as mundane as a type of endangered cricket. Then there are laws stemming from the Animal Welfare Act, the Migratory Bird Treaty of 1918, and dozens of others.

After you've leapt all those hurdles, you may then choose to get your zoo accredited by the Association of Zoos and Aquariums, yet another monumental (but at least optional) endeavor. The AZA was founded in 1924 as the American Association of Zoological Parks and Aquariums and is currently based in Silver Spring, Maryland, not far from where I myself grew up. Think of it as the "seal of approval" (no pun intended) for zoos, with accredited parks required to meet a much higher standard in the fields of animal care, conservation, and research than unaccredited institutions.

Achieving accreditation with the AZA is no simple task. Prospective zoos must first pass a vigorous inspection carried out by three AZA experts in various animal-related fields. If that initial inspection is passed, then your application is submitted to a panel of twelve other experts

for review. It is here that the decision is made as to whether or not to label your zoo an AZA-accredited zoo. If the accreditation is awarded, the standards must be held or else you risk losing it in five years, when mandatory repeat inspections are performed.

It's an arduous process, but one whose reward carries a good deal of prestige. It's such a difficult achievement, in fact, that fewer than 10% of the world's zoos and aquariums carry the distinction.

Once you've built your park, gotten your licenses and imported your animals, possibly earned AZA accreditation, and pulled half of your hair out, the real challenges can begin.

Zoo maintenance is an absolute logistical nightmare. An army of accountants is required just to balance the food budget for the park's animals. Not to mention that a vast majority of zoo operations has absolutely zero to do with its actual fauna. This includes staff for operating guest shops, cleaning, landscaping, and doctors to attend to guests and staff who may have ventured a little too close to the animals. And don't even begin to think about the insurance, especially if you plan on housing dangerous predators such as saltwater crocodiles or giant monster sharks.

From the original zoo concept, many sub-varieties have sprouted. Safari parks, such as those in San Diego, California or Asheboro, North Carolina, allow visitors to drive amongst large animals such as giraffes and zebras. Petting zoos offer smaller, cuter options such as donkeys or pigs for children (or child-like adults (me)) to pet and play with.

Many zoos are barely zoos at all. In an effort to maximize exposure and cast a wide net over a larger demographic, hybrid amusement park-zoos can be found all over the world, and most notably in the United States and Japan. These venues, such as Busch Gardens in Tampa or any of the SeaWorld locations, combine the roller coasters and games of an amusement park with sections of the park dedicated to displaying their menageries, usually at the cost of a single ticket. Hershey Park in Pennsylvania is a lesser known example, with one side of its park containing rides and the other a small zoo.

But one of the more popular types of zoo—that's almost as old as the standard zoological park itself—is the aquarium.

We can look outside any time and see birds, or squirrels, and grass and trees. The terrestrial world is ours. It's our home and we are accustomed to it. The world beneath the waves, however, is completely alien to us. That may be one of the reasons that public aquariums are just as popular, if not more so, than many public zoos. They offer glimpses into a domain we'd otherwise never see, with creatures so extraordinary that they surpass our imaginations.

The concept of keeping fish in enclosures for display is a concept as old as the Roman Empire. It is believed that the first fish to be successfully kept in captivity was the Mediterranean barbel, *Barbus meridionalis,* which is a bottom dweller much like catfish. The fish were kept as pets in marble bowls, and most likely were only able to survive such stagnant conditions due to their hardy nature.

In 50 AD, glass panes became a common fixture in Roman society, and they were soon used in conjunction with marble boxes to create the first real fish tanks—or aquariums—as we know today.

It can be argued that the modern look of home aquariums, the kind you see at pet shops, can be owed to the *Wardian case*, invented by Nathaniel Ward in the early 1800s. The Wardian case was simply a sealed glass container primarily used for plants, though modified later by Dr. Ward to hold water and aquatic animals.

Keeping aquariums became a popular hobby in the mid-19th century, and eventually the very first public aquarium was opened in the London Zoo. It was known as the Fish House. (The word "aquarium" is a shortened version of "aquatic vivarium.")

In 1908, a mechanical air pump was invented for use in water. This allowed hobbyists to aerate the water and keep fish healthier. After World War I, when electricity became more commonplace, aquariums were able to utilize artificial lighting, filtration systems, and heating elements, allowing for more exotic inhabitants. This led to more impressive displays and a higher demand for aquarium products, and in turn more complex public aquariums.

As public aquariums grew in popularity, their need to "push the envelope," so to speak, did as well. Goldfish and pike and clams were no longer enough to satisfy guests, so many modern aquariums have turned to larger and more impressive specimens. Nearly every SeaWorld park houses multiple killer whales (though that program is ending at the time of this book's writing), dolphins are a common sight, giant octopuses are a mainstay, and the Georgia Aquarium at one point was even home to *four* enormous whale sharks—the largest fish in the sea.

So it was only inevitable that SeaLand of Myrtle Beach would eventually attempt to join the crowded list of popular aquariums throughout the United States with its own star attraction. Founded in 1996, SeaLand was home to about 5,000 different animals, including a family of otters and at one point a large killer whale. However, it had been drowned out by Myrtle Beach's oversaturated entertainment scene and was hemorrhaging money by the spring of 2015. Around this time is when the region was devastated by Tropical Storm Ana.

And it would be the catalyst for one of the most infamous chain of events in the history of aquariums.

3
Like it Was Meant to Be

Tropical Storm Ana is really who we have to thank for this mess," said James Warren as we sat at a bar made out of a red sailboat. The exterior hull served as the counter while a bartender walked around the inside, serving drinks and taking food orders. We were at one of the most popular restaurants in Myrtle Beach, the Giant Crab Seafood Restaurant. It's a colorful place, with nautical-themed décor everywhere you look and a bright blue color palette. Outside is a giant statue of a smiling red crab in a sea captain's hat to appease the kids and give the place its unique charm.

An hour before, I was sitting in James Warren's small office at the SeaLand of Myrtle Beach park. I was expecting something vast and open, with perhaps a giant glass wall offering a view of the ocean. Instead, it was just a little corner office with plain white walls and no larger than the smallest bedroom in my little house. There were no signs of nefariousness or corporate greed; just pictures of his wife and son and lots of nature magazines and a single filing cabinet upon which were stacked some empty foam takeout boxes.

I was scheduled to meet with Warren at three in the afternoon, but apparently a prior meeting had gone hours later than he was expecting and he was late. He was both apologetic and hungry, and offered me an early dinner at one of Myrtle Beach's most beloved dining spots. Soon after, we were sitting at the boat bar, sipping Coronas while snacking on buffalo shrimp and crab cakes.

James Warren was a powerful-looking man, especially with the sleeves of his dress shirt rolled up. He could've easily been a linebacker or a boxer. He'd grown up in urban Detroit in the 1970s and 1980s in poverty. From an early age, he felt very different from his peers in that he was more interested in academic pursuits than the street life he'd been surrounded by. On full scholarship to Old Dominion University in Norfolk, Virginia, Warren received Bachelor's degrees in both oceanography and business management, or as he put it, "One for his passion and one for his future."

Over the next twenty years, he'd be involved in a number of activist groups, most of them dealing with conservation. Ten years ago, he and a group of other African American businessmen opened up a small science museum for children in Detroit, for which he was honored by the NAACP. He'd also been involved in the Myrtle Beach community since his arrival in 2002, when he was named the Director of Operations for SeaLand.

James Warren had been painted by the media as a villain in the aftermath of the SeaLand incident. The incident, as so many were quick to announce, was supposedly the product of Warren's greed. The image that came to mind was of a shadowy cloaked figure overlooking a darkened boardroom table of similarly-dressed executives, all tapping their fingertips together in wicked glee. From what had been written, I was expecting the kind of man who'd be played by

Danny Devito in a pinstriped suit, complete with a monocle and maniacal, psychotic cackle as he rolled around in his blood money.

But I can tell you, from a purely objective standpoint, that wasn't true at all.

James Warren spent the first fifteen minutes of my interview wiping buffalo sauce from his goatee and talking about his son's soccer tournaments. He talked about some of SeaLand's recent conservation efforts and personally volunteering for various trips. He talked about expanding the park and adding employees and hiring more researchers.

He never once talked about money.

While true, he would later admit, that SeaLand's primary goal with the acquisition of the Great White shark was financial, it was more of a means to an end. "You can't save the planet without money," he would say in an interview with Vogue. "At the end of the day, SeaLand's goal is to raise awareness and fund conservation efforts. You can't do either of those things to very great extent without the financial ability to do so."

At the time, nobody wanted to admit that he was right. Philanthropy was impossible without money, something SeaLand had been sorely lacking.

"We couldn't compete with all the other attractions at Myrtle Beach that offered a more…colorful experience," he told me with a hint of disdain in his voice. "Here we have IMAX theaters, putt-putt courses on every corner, God knows how many restaurants, the boardwalk, everything. An aquarium, especially one as small as ours, got lost in the shuffle. And then you have all this media surrounding killer whales, which didn't exactly help."

Keeping killer whales in captivity was a hot-button issue. In one sense, the whales owe their fame, and subsequently many of the conservation efforts surrounding them, to shows such as SeaWorld's Shamu show. But visitor interest in whales had been steadily waning for years, perhaps reaching its lowest point with the release of the 2013 documentary *Blackfish*.

Blackfish told the story of Tilikum, a killer whale that had spent most of its life in captivity. Tilikum had been responsible for the deaths of numerous trainers, and the makers of the documentary had used such incidents as points of emphasis against keeping killer whales. They argue, in a nutshell, that the ethical costs outweigh any benefits.

As a result of the popularity of *Blackfish*, many marine parks began ending their killer whale programs. In 2016, SeaWorld announced that they'd end captive breeding and eventually end the show entirely (though whether the captive whales would be reintroduced to the wild remains to be seen at the time of this piece).

While the morality of captive killer whales is ultimately up the reader, it is important, I feel, to mention the Miami Seaquarium. Something James Warren brought up.

"The killer whales?" I asked him, pushing away a plate of oysters. I never liked oysters. To me, it was no different from eating snot. The only oyster I'd had was actually by accident. A friend and I were wandering downtown Columbia, South Carolina when we were offered oyster shooters at a local bar. I thought it was just a clever name, but it turned out that it *actually* contained a live oyster, something I didn't learn until I'd felt it in my mouth with horror.

"The pressure to end killer whale captivity programs," Warren explained. "You know," he sighed, "that's one of those things where you sort of had to teach yourself to take the bad with the good. Look, don't get me wrong here, I can completely understand why the idea of keeping such a big animal in what equates to a fish bowl can be morally challenging, but the reality is that many of the conservation programs that exist today are only around because of captive orcas capturing the public's imagination.

"The problem is that for every park that did it right, two more did it wrong," he continued, swigging his beer. "We took pride in our orca's health and happiness as much as anything else. Unfortunately, there are a lot of irresponsible parks out there, and of course everyone with a Twitter account thinks they're an activist because they repost something someone else wrote."

SeaLand hosted a killer whale—Darcy—for six years. About eight months before Tropical Storm Ana, Darcy was released back into the wild after Warren and the park bowed to pressure from activists. For eight months before the storm, her tank stood empty.

Warren continued, "But too many parks care more about putting on a show than they do about the welfare of their animals. Especially the [expletive that rhymes with "ducking"] Seaquarium." He shook his head in disgust.

He went on to tell me about the deplorable conditions faced by the Miami Seaquarium's resident orca, Lolita. Lolita has lived at the park since 1970 and is kept in a tank that to you or I would feel no bigger than a small cubicle. Her tank, known as the Whale Bowl (or the Goldfish Bowl, if you were an activist), is only 35 feet wide and 20 feet deep. Taken at face value, the dimensions of Lolita's tank don't exactly seem diminutive, but it is imperative to realize that Lolita herself is 21 feet long.

The Animal and Plant Health Inspection Service (APHIS) currently operates under the USDA and sets guidelines for various habitat sizes to be used in park exhibits. According to APHIS guidelines, a killer whale's tank should be no less than 48 feet wide in either direction. Lolita's tank clearly violates this standard by an uncomfortably vast margin.

"The standards," Warren said, "are set by the average size of the cetacean group [whales and dolphins]. Killer whales are considered Group One cetaceans and as a species they average twenty-four feet long, that means that the absolute minimum width of their tank has to be *double* that. That's the *minimum*. Our pool is sixty feet, and thirty feet at its deepest point. We went above and beyond with our orca. Seaquarium, unfortunately, doesn't."

"Wait," I interjected, "why is the Seaquarium allowed to violate the standards?" Warren had mentioned that, according to APHIS, any tanks in violation of the spacing requirements had to be modified to accommodate them. So it made no sense that the Seaquarium could get away with it.

He answered *emphatically*, "Because the [expletives] are measuring it differently than the rest of the world and eschewing common sense." He went on to elaborate: Lolita's pool contains a "work island" in the middle. This island is essentially the top, above-water part of a narrow divider that extends nearly the width of the tank. It provides an area for the trainers to interact with Lolita without actually getting in the water. Behind the work island is more water, but it's impossible for Lolita to get to it without going around the work island, and most of that water is quarantined off for a couple of Pacific white-sided dolphins (*Lagenorhynchus obliquidens*). Miami Seaquarium, when making their measurements, included the total length of the pool *without* taking the giant work island/wall, which divides it roughly in half, into consideration.

"Imagine you're building a house with an architect and you say that a room has to be ten feet long," Warren said. "Well, the architect builds your room, but then puts up a huge divider than spans almost the entire width, leaving a gap of a foot or two on each side."

"I'd be pretty pissed," I tell him.

"Most people would. Now imagine that the architect insists that the room is ten feet. 'Yeah,' he says, 'there is a divider, but the room itself is ten feet.' And those are the official measurements, and there's nothing in the contract that says he *couldn't* put a dividing wall there. Seaquarium has been that asshole contractor, and they've gotten away with it based off that ridiculous technicality."

The Miami Seaquarium responded to the growing criticism concerning the size of Lolita's tank by stating that her tank was 60 feet long, like SeaLand's, and that it exceeded the minimum. Of course, it was measured without including the giant wall in the middle.

"It's a damn shame," Warren reiterated. "Hopefully they'll come to their senses. That whale deserves better."

Now, the cynic in me would, under most circumstances, believe that James Warren was putting on a show for me. He knew I was writing this piece about the SeaLand incident, and obviously wanted to appear sympathetic. But it's difficult to put into words, even for a so-called professional writer, the deep, earnest tone with which Warren spoke of his hatred for the Miami Seaquarium's treatment of Lolita. This was not a man telling me what he thought my readers wanted to hear. This was a man telling me how he truly felt. His passion for the animals under his watch, to me at least, was completely genuine.

"So killer whales are off the board, but giant sharks are okay?" I asked, not meaning to question his ethics but out of genuine interest in this supposed double standard.

"Whales, especially killer whales," he said, "are humanized a lot more than sharks. Whales are intelligent creatures. While sharks aren't exactly dumb, they aren't the sharpest tools in the shed, either. They're essentially big eating machines. You won't teach a shark to do tricks. As an animal of much lower intelligence that needs far less mental stimulation, we didn't think it was as morally bankrupt to keep one in a tank, especially such a large tank. We kept the shark in Darcy's old tank, and since the shark was considerably smaller [than Darcy], it had a lot of room."

"You mentioned humanizing. Did public image have anything to do with the...uh...decision?"

"Oh, absolutely." Warren was more honest than I had been expecting. "You have to take PR [sic] into consideration when making a decision like we made. Sharks attract a lot of conservation efforts, for sure, but nothing on the scale of whales. There are entire reality shows dedicated to saving whales from poachers. Meanwhile sharks are hunted by the thousands and no one bats an eye. The general public, for the most part, sees sharks as monsters, which is something we hoped to change with our exhibit. So we felt more comfortable from a public relations standpoint attempting to house a Great White than a killer whale."

Warren had referenced the practice of capturing sharks to make shark fin soup, a luxury food item popular in China that is exactly what it sounds like. The shark's rough fins give the soup a unique texture that's highly valued by Chinese restaurants. Shark fins are collected through a process called "finning," wherein sharks are caught by the hundreds, their fins culled while still alive, and then tossed back into the ocean to slowly die of suffocation or be eaten alive by other predators.

Shark finning is undoubtedly a horrendous practice that only exists for revenue. Collecting only the profitable parts of the shark and then tossing the rest back instead of using valuable storage space on a vessel has allowed the enterprise to flourish. Nonetheless, some countries have taken steps to curtail such a barbaric procedure by requiring harvesters to bring the entire shark back to the mainland before collecting the fins instead of leaving it to an arduous death. Finning is completely prohibited in the United States, where the demand is low anyway.

Sadly, however, there is relatively little resistance to finning compared to many other conservation efforts. There was a documentary in 2007 called *Sharkwater* that exposed the practice, but it wasn't met with the same fanfare as *Blackfish* and thus had little impact. The justification for the lack of finning laws purportedly has to do with the suggestion that sharks will be caught accidentally en masse regardless, so they might as well be used.

"We have to tread water very lightly in this climate," Warren said as he finished his second beer and ordered another. "Internet activism has gotten out of hand. Everyone wants to feel like they're a part of some heroic movement, so they have to look under rocks and nooks and crannies to find villains. And when they can't find one, they make them up. Sometimes, hell, *most* of the time, that means either exaggerating a transgression or ignoring any evidence that goes against the viewpoint they already decided they have."

"Hashtag culture," I nodded, slightly embarrassed by my own status as a millennial and our penchant for uninformed mob justice.

"It's a double-edged sword," Warren went on. "Activism can be great. It can lead to fantastic things. You and I probably wouldn't be here talking if it not for the civil rights movements of the [nineteen] sixties. But the problem is that we live in such a comparatively comfortable world now, and people are so *desperate* to have *something* to rally against, that they dig up trivial things or take things out of context or purposely 'misinterpret' something just to give themselves something to be mad about. Do you know what one of the first major PR issues we had to deal with was?"

I shrugged. I had assumed that "keeping a gigantic monster shark in a fish bowl" would be one of the first punching bags for public outcry.

"We named our shark Brody. You know, Chief Brody." Chief Martin Brody was the name of the protagonist of *Jaws*. I thought it was a clever homage when I first heard it myself. Such an innocent name, too, for such a dangerous animal. "Brody was a male shark. So we named it Brody. Who cares, right? Apparently lots of people. I can't tell you how many emails we got chewing us out for assigning the shark a gender role. A *shark*. *With male genitalia.* We were being ridiculed by half a dozen social justice groups, most organized by college students pretending to be oppressed and throwing the term 'microaggression' around like it was going out of style, because we had given our male shark a traditionally male name."

He laughed and shook his head. "I couldn't believe it. I thought it was a freaking joke. But it wasn't. They were dead serious. They made Twitter things, started Facebook groups, all because of what we named our shark, and their supposed interpretation that we were being purposely exclusive to certain individuals. Ridiculous." He rolled his eyes. "All of the problems in the world—starvation, homelessness, wage gaps—and *this* is what some people decided was the world's greatest evil. Call me a jerk, call me whatever you want, call me an 'evil republican,' but I just don't see the benefit of making mountains out of molehills just for the sake of having something to be angry about. People have this innate need to see the world in black and white, good and evil. Your side is wrong and my side is right. But it's not. The world is gray. And people aren't comfortable with that reality. So they refuse to accept it in favor of their own."

Gender fluidity, identity, and LGBT politics had arguably reached a level in 2015 they'd never reached before, and for the better. While you won't catch me picketing films that don't include LGBT characters, I do sympathize with most of the causes highlighted by the movement, provided that forums actually have meaningful dialogue and not name-calling (a rarity, unfortunately). Discussing sexual politics is outside the scope of this piece, but Warren's point was thus: people will find problems when they *want* to find problems.

"But you can't win," Warren said. "Are we supposed to give the shark a traditional girl's name, and then be accused of feminizing certain names? The goalposts always move with some social activists. You're damned if you do, damned if you don't. Me, me, me. The only way not to lose is to not play the game."

So SeaLand refused to play the game. As a result of the "outrage" over *daring* to give their male shark a masculine name, they posted a bulletin on their website stating that they understood the activists' concerns and would take them into consideration, which of course they never did. The decision had already been made and fliers were already being printed.

I made a brief mention to Warren that we'd gotten a little off topic and he apologized. I asked him about Tropical Storm Ana and how that resulted in SeaLand deciding to house a Great White shark—an animal thought impossible to keep in captivity for any significant length of time.

It all had to do with Murrell's Inlet.

Murrell's Inlet is a body of water about twenty minutes south of the Myrtle Beach tourist strip. It's a small but affluent community known for its famed Biker Bar (actual name) and expensive waterfront homes. The inlet itself extends into the mainland like a tentacle of seawater, providing a place for dozens of homes to dock their boats. The inlet, which rarely exceeds 15 feet in depth, eventually turns into a swampy saltmarsh surrounded by a boardwalk and restaurants.

"Imagine a small bay," Warren said when describing the main creek of Murrell's Inlet. "Its shore is dotted with homes and each one has a dock. It's connected by a mouth approximately two hundred feet wide and protected by two jetties."

I had some rudimentary knowledge of jetties. My grandparents had a house on the Chesapeake Bay in Maryland and growing up I'd play on the jetty, but never really knew what it was for. I played dumb (sort of) and asked Warren what he meant by jetties.

"The jetties are sort of like protective walls made of rock. They're situated on each side of the mouth of the inlet and stretch out into the water in parallel. Imagine, um," he scoured the bar and found two straws, "that my mouth is the mouth of Murrell's Inlet, connected to the ocean."

"Okay…"

"The reason that mouth exists is because there's a gap in the coastline. But longshore drift means that gap—that channel—could close over time, and the residents need that channel to stay open so they can get their boats in and out. So the solution? Jetties." He stuck both straws in his mouth, one on each side, jutting outward.

I nodded and tried not to chuckle.

After removing the straws from his mouth (and thankfully not putting them back in the straw cup), he went on to explain that longshore drift was exactly what it sounded like: the "drifting" of sand, clay, and other sediments along coastlines. The mechanisms behind this process are extraordinarily complex and require headache-inducing formulas to fully understand. In a nutshell, however, sediments are carried by waves, which are then deposited onto beaches ("deposition") in swash.

"You know when you're standing at the beach, right at the water's edge?" Warren asked. "That small layer of water that rushes up to your ankles then subsides back into the ocean is known as *swash*, and it's what deposits sediment on the beach. Over time, enough sediment piles up to where new beaches are formed, or the mouths of inlets are closed, or lagoons are made, or spits, or any number of possibilities. These effects are of course exacerbated by faster moving water, like the kind brought out by storms or hurricanes."

That was the day I learned that the little breaking wave that no one pays attention to actually had a proper name. I'd make sure on my next beach trip to smugly point out to my wife and daughter that it was called "swash."

James Warren once taught high school oceanography, and his expertise was showing. (Though it's possible that I could have just been so ignorant on the subject that he could easily just be making things up.) An anecdote he'd tell me in subsequent conversations involved the number of kids who'd transfer out of his class after the first day. There seemed to be an omnipresent belief among the uninitiated that oceanography and marine biology are interchangeable. They're not. So kids would sign up for his class thinking they'd get to learn about fish or dolphins and penguins, only to instead to read a syllabus encompassing coastal erosion, subduction zones, and currents.

"Oceanography," he told me shortly before I finished the first draft of this piece, "is basically geology. Hydrology, to be more appropriate. How does the ocean work? It's relatively boring when compared to marine biology, which is the study of the things that live in that ocean. Kids aren't as into it. But it grows on you."

Tropical Storm Ana formed on May 8, 2015 and was the earliest storm of its kind to make landfall in the United States (in any given year). By May 10th, it had made landfall along the beaches of South Carolina, with peak winds reaching 60 miles per hour.

Ana was, in the grand scheme of hurricane history, relatively minor. It caused minimal damage in the form of some downed trees and power lines and only a bit of flooding in North Myrtle Beach. In fact, many considered the rain it brought to be relatively beneficial, as the Carolinas had been experiencing a minor drought at the time. All in all, Ana's impact wasn't entirely noteworthy.

With the exception of course being what it had done to Murrell's Inlet.

"The jetties," Warren said, "were designed to keep sand drifting down from the beaches out of the channel. That way the channel would never be closed and boats could go in and out. But call it a fluke of nature, call it what you want, but I'll be damned if a sandbar didn't appear the next day anyway. It barely reached the surface, but it stretched across the entire channel, basically closing the inlet off from the ocean."

Sandbars, or shoals, are naturally-forming ridges created by sediment deposition. Waves come in, move large bodies of sediment, and it builds up into a sandbar. It isn't unusual for sandbars to form overnight after a heavy storm. In fact, when I was working in an office near Charlotte, North Carolina, we had a pond out back. After an unusually violent storm, we arrived the next day to find that a small peninsula had formed, stretching out almost to the center of the pond. This is because the heavy rains and wind made waves that deposited sediment that had up until then been dispersed evenly throughout the bottom of the pond in one place, forming the sandbar.

"Tropical Storm Ana," Warren told me, "turned Murrell's

Inlet into Murrell's Lagoon. Despite the jetties, it was now closed off from the ocean."

"How do you think that happened?" I asked.

"Damned if we know, to be honest. But we have an idea." Warren then explained that the most likely reason that the sandbar was able to form, despite the jetties blocking coastal sand from reaching—then subsequently building up in—the mouth of the inlet, was because the cyclonic nature of Ana's winds pushed the waves *outward*, toward the ocean. Typically, longshore drift occurred when waves pushed against the coastline, depositing any sediment they carried in swash. However, Ana reversed this as it struck the mainland, and the sediments dispersed throughout the bottom of Murrell's Inlet built up near the mouth.

"The jetties worked wonders at keeping the ocean's and beach's sediments out of the mouth of the inlet, but because of Ana, instead sediments that were already *in* the inlet were able to build up and block off the exit."

In most other circumstances, this wouldn't have been a huge deal. Excavators would've been called, the sandbar would've been cleared, and the wealthy boat owners would've been able to sail in and out of the inlet at their leisure within days.

But this was no ordinary circumstance.

"We got a call from Myrtle Beach Animal Control the day after the storm subsided. A guy living along the main creek of Murrell's Inlet had gone out to check on his boat when he saw the silhouette of a sixteen-foot shark swimming around his dock. He was scared out of his mind and had to lock up his dog, which kept trying to jump into the water after it. The damn shark must have swum into the inlet and it closed up in the storm before it left, so it got stuck."

A shark getting caught in lakes, rivers, estuaries or inlets is not a new phenomenon. In fact, it is actually quite common. Sharks can be found in lakes all over the world, usually after finding their way there after a flood. Some can even be found swimming far upriver. A rather interesting golf course in Australia, as a matter of fact, is home to an entire population of bull sharks, *Carcharhinus leucas*, that became stranded after floodwaters had receded.

"The homeowner had called the police," Warren said, "who then called animal control, who then called us. Guess they didn't have the expertise to go in for it. Can you imagine the look on the animal control guy's face? Great Whites are typically open ocean sharks, so it's rare to see one near the shore let alone have one swim into an inlet, *let alone* have a tropical storm completely seal that inlet shortly after."

I nodded. The odds were incredibly slim.

"It's like it was meant to be," Warren chuckled. "We just so happened to have an empty tank thanks to releasing our killer whale. It was dry at that time, but we were able to talk to the local government and get the process of filling it expedited."

The tanks of public aquariums are often filled with municipal water. SeaLand was no different. There was no specialized imported water. The water seen in the tanks was the same that came out of everyone's faucets, albeit infused with salt and other chemicals to mimic seawater. Other aquariums pulled water directly from the ocean. For example, the South Carolina Aquarium collects water from the Charleston Harbor for use in its exhibits. For this reason, many aquariums are built near the shoreline.

Warren continued. "We diverted our contractors that were working on a new gift shop and had them work overtime to patch up Darcy's old tank, but that was just the start. After the decision had been made and the approvals granted, we just had to figure out how to get the shark there. That was a logistical nightmare in and of itself."

The details of said nightmare will be explained in detail later in this piece—as well as the process by which SeaLand executives, Warren included, came to their rushed (and ultimately tragic) decision. However, for the moment, I had no doubt about how excited James Warren was for the incredible opportunity that had bestowed itself upon his little park. They had it all planned out; they were going to attempt something that had never been done before.

But even the best laid plans go astray.

4

A Million Little Variables

odern home aquariums arguably owe their existence to a man named Robert Warrington. His aquariums in the 1800s consisted of glass panels, held together with wire frames and putty, with a floor of metal. To keep the temperatures up, flames were lit below the tanks, heating the metal and thus the water. Today, we have much more sophisticated techniques that are not only more efficient but don't run the risk of turning your aquarium's inhabitants into soup.

A simple freshwater aquarium typically consists of three components: a filter, a light, and a heater. The water in an aquarium must be constantly cleaned to remove harmful phosphates and ammonia, which result from the inhabitants needing to inevitably defecate. Though there are many different kinds of filters, the typical filter you'd find on most starter aquarium kits use an inlet pipe to suck up water, push it through a filter medium, then pump it back into the tank via a spillway. The filter medium not only captures organic particles, but also contains activated carbon that neutralizes ammonia (turning it to nitrate).

Heaters are necessary for tropical tanks, which usually require water temperatures between 77 and 82 degrees

Fahrenheit. Aquarium heaters usually consists of a tube-like heating element encased in glass with a thermostat inside, heating up whenever the water gets too cool much like the programmable thermostats in many peoples' homes. In some setups, aquarium keepers may surround the heater with a wire mesh to prevent their less-intelligent fish from sitting against it and burning themselves. On the opposite side of the coin, an aquarium chiller may also be used if attempting to house coldwater fish.

Lights are technically optional, but a nice touch. Lights used for most simple freshwater aquariums are just standard fluorescent tube lights that produce very little heat and therefore don't directly affect the water temperature.

And there you have it. A simple freshwater setup. While a far cry from the fish bowls of yesteryear, they're still nothing fancy and relatively easy to maintain. (Fish bowls, incidentally, are not ideal for any fish with the exception of certain Siamese fighting fish, or bettas, because of their ability to breathe surface air.)

"Freshwater is easy, though," said Julius Vang of FinsUp, a large pet shop in Baltimore, Maryland specializing in—you guessed it—fish. "Marine [saltwater] aquariums are a completely different ballgame." I was in town to visit the National Aquarium in Baltimore to learn some of the more technical aspects of housing large sharks, or creating gigantic saltwater tanks, when I decided to stop into the store and see how it's done on a smaller scale first. I'd spoken to one of the employees, who was more than happy to give me a tour and some lessons, provided I mentioned his name in this book. As you can see, I kept up my end of the bargain, and luckily so did he.

Anna Thynne, a British zoologist, built history's first saltwater aquarium in 1846. Her setup was very simple, at least for a marine aquarium, and contained only sponges and corals. It is believed that she used water right from the ocean, and was able to maintain a balanced ecosystem in her marine aquariums for well over three years, an incredible feat for the time.

It wasn't until the 1950s that marine aquariums really became mainstream. It took advances in filtration technology and a better understanding of marine environments, most notably water chemistry, in order to make marine aquariums more widespread among hobbyists.

"A saltwater tank essentially works the same as a freshwater tank," Vang explained, "but it's a much more fragile ecosystem, especially when it comes to the water." Originally, he explained, saltwater for marine aquariums almost exclusively came straight from the ocean. As such, inland saltwater tanks were extraordinarily rare until the invention of synthetic seawater, created using a chemically-balanced salt mix.

The difference between freshwater fish and saltwater fish comes down to a process called osmoregulation, with *osmo* meaning "water" and *regulation* meaning, uh, "regulation." Osmoregulation, in very unscientific terms, is essentially the movement of water in and out of cells; in this case the cells of an aquatic creature. If the cells have too much water, they'll explode. Too little, and they'll shrivel and die of dehydration. Neither outcome is exactly desirable, so aquatic organisms have developed a way to maintain homeostasis—balance—within their cells.

A vast majority of aquatic animals are stenohaline,

meaning that they can either thrive in saltwater environments or freshwater environments, but not both. Freshwater fish suck water in through their gills, which is why you always see them flapping in tanks, and extract any traces of salt they can find. Because freshwater obviously contains much smaller concentrations of salt than saltwater, freshwater fish are almost constantly urinating to expel all the excess water they need to take on. Marine fish are the exact opposite. Because the salt content of their bodies is less than the surrounding water, they're at risk of having too much salt and not enough water, so salt particles are *expelled* through their gills in order to maintain balance.

While rare, there are fish and other aquatic organisms that actually do well in both environments. These are known as euryhaline animals, and include salmon, some types of stingrays, and the infamous bull shark—which is how a population of them was able to survive on that Australian golf course. These fish can typically be found closer to coastlines or in estuaries, where freshwater and saltwater mix, leading to a wide range of salinities at any given time in any given spot.

"What happens if you put a freshwater fish in a saltwater tank?" I asked Julius.

"It'll be like pouring salt on a slug. It'll dehydrate."

"Dehydrate underwater?" That seemed like one of those cuckoo, bizzaro kinks in physics more appropriate for episodes of *Spongebob* than real life.

"Freshwater fish are built to keep as much salt as possible," Julius said. "They have no way to expel it." He went on to explain that freshwater fish lacked the biological mechanism to eliminate excess salt because it wasn't an issue they normally had to deal with. As such, a freshwater fish in a saltwater environment would take on so much salt that their cells would shrivel and die. Conversely, a saltwater fish placed in freshwater will expel too much salt (as they're used to) and take on too much water, so their cells would oversaturate and explode.

"I sort of figured water was just water," I said, playing dumb. Of course, I do a lot of preliminary research before most articles of this nature, but I also like to get as many facts quoted as possible from experts.

"Not at all," Julius shook his head. "Animals, us included, live in mediums. Think about air for a second. Without it we die, obviously, but think about what it is." In more scientific terms than Julies offered, his point was that the air we breathe is not "just air," as I thought water was "just water." Our natural breathing air is actually a very precise chemical cocktail of oxygen (21%) nitrogen (78%) and argon (around 1%) with trace amounts of other gases. There are other types of breathing gases, with oxygen being the common and most vital denominator, that are generated for use in different scenarios. Heliox, for example, is a mixture of oxygen and helium, with no nitrogen, used for deep dives to prevent nitrogen narcosis. There are many others, all containing different mixtures, including Trimix, Hydrox and Nitrox.

"The medium we live in is just as fragile as the one fish live in," Julius said. "If suddenly all the oxygen was removed from our atmosphere, even for a few seconds, we'd all be brain dead. So obviously when dealing with fish, we have to treat the water just like we'd treat our atmosphere, in that we have to get it right to keep the fish alive."

"So explain to me the basic differences between a saltwater and freshwater tank," I asked of him.

The first answer was obvious: one contains freshwater and one contains saltwater. No need for much of a brain on that one. However, the differences between fresh and marine environments were numerous and complex, yet often oversimplified by peasants such as myself.

Julius told me a humorous story from back in 2003, when the film *Finding Nemo* made keeping common clownfish, *Amphiprion ocellaris*, immensely popular. "There was a woman walking around with a fish bowl we sold for bettas and goldfish who said she wanted a clownfish. I told her you couldn't put it in a bowl. She asked why and I told her that it was because it was a saltwater fish. Then she said 'Okay so then where's the salt?' in a really condescending way."

You can't just use Morton's salt, the kind you buy in tubs at the grocery store, in a marine aquarium. It doesn't work that way, as Julius explained. There are a million little variables to consider when creating the perfect batch of fish-safe saltwater, some of which Julius was kind enough to go over and dumb down for me.

"Specific gravity is usually the first thing we look for when we set up a tank and fill it up. That tells us how dense the water is," he explained. "For an FO tank, you want it between one point zero two zero [1.020] and one point zero two four [1.024]. For a reef tank you want it a little bit higher." FO tanks are shorthand for "Fish Only" tanks in the home aquarium world. These tanks, as their name implies, contain only living fish and everything else, including the corals and plants, is artificial, and therefore not bounded to the stricter environmental parameters that must be maintained otherwise. The other two types of tanks are FOWLR tanks, or "Fish Only With Live Rock," and reef tanks, which contain live corals. Live rock is a porous rock that contains hundreds of thousands of microscopic invertebrates that will eventually be lunch for some of the aquarium's larger inhabitants.

"The second thing we need to look for is the salinity," Julius said. Standing near a row of aquariums in the store, he dipped what looked like a little graduated cylinder into one of the tanks and filled it with water, then lifted it to eye level. Inside was a little bobber that pointed to a marked line. This is known as a hygrometer, and is used to measure both salinity and specific gravity. "The salinity of this tank is about thirty-one PPT [31 ppt]. That's right where we want it to be." In an ideal marine environment, the salinity level is between 28 and 35 ppt, or "parts per trillion." "You can get away with a little higher in larger reef systems since the bigger the tank, the less fluctuation there is in the water conditions and less chance of systemic shock."

What Julius had described will come into play later, upon my visit to some gigantic shark tanks a few miles away. Systemic shock is the sudden change in an environment that causes the organisms in that environment to die off. Though it may seem to be the opposite of what one might expect, larger aquariums are actually much more chemically stable than smaller aquariums. Drop a cup of poison in a tiny one-gallon tank and it will change the whole environment. Drop the same cup in a tank with a hundred thousand gallons and it makes almost no difference whatsoever.

"Next is the pH level," Julius went on. "You typically

want to keep it around eight point three [8.3], unlike freshwater fish which like a more neutral environment."

"How do you raise or lower the pH?" I asked. "I get the salt. If it's too low, just add more." He then made sure to tell me, before I went on, that saltwater is always mixed *away* from a tank and then poured in. Pouring marine salt directly into an aquarium will burn the inhabitants' gills off. "But the pH is just the alkalinity, right? Isn't that sort of set in stone by the water company or whatever? Does the salt raise it?"

"Two ways, really." He reached into the nearby tank and grazed a fine layer of sharp white pebbles at the bottom. A few clownfish darted out of the way of his hand. "Calcium-rich substrate on the bottom helps raise the pH. There are also buffering agents that contain special chemicals which can help raise it."

"I see."

"So the last things all should be kept as low as possible, and that's stuff like copper, phosphates, nitrates and ammonia."

"How can ammonia spike in a tank, besides urination?"

"When a fish dies and its body breaks down, it floods the tank with ammonia, which is lethal. The filters can remove a lot of it, but it can act fast, so if we see a fish has died, we scoop it out right away. We usually have regular checks."

I'd have to remember this for later. If dead organic matter created ammonia spikes in a tank, then how exactly did they feed Brody, who lived off organic matter in very large quantities, without that being an issue? The answer, as it would turn out, would be related to the systemic shock mentioned earlier. Because Brody the Great White's pool at SeaLand was so large, ammonia spikes weren't detrimental to the overall water quality, at least not to any significant degree. However, that would be explored later.

I thanked Julius for the quick lesson on saltwater aquariums. I knew a lot more then than I did before I walked in, and hopefully it'd help me not feel so much like an idiot during my next interview, with Dr. Peter Bradford of the National Aquarium. I had learned the basics of how small home saltwater aquariums worked. Now I needed to know how they worked on a much, *much* larger scale.

B altimore's National Aquarium is one of the world's preeminent non-profit public aquariums. It was completed in 1981 right in the Maryland city's beautiful inner harbor on the Chesapeake Bay, near the edge of downtown. The facility houses over 17,000 specimens from over 700 different species and attracts in excess of a million and a half visitors every year. I actually volunteered here for a week when I was in high school and still remember having to wear the same blue polo and white khaki shorts every day.

The aquarium is actually composed of three separate buildings. All of them are connected to each other, with the first and second being side by side. The third is connected to the second via a raised walkway stretching over a channel between the piers serving as the facility's foundations.

The first building, or at least the one usually visited first, is made almost entirely of glass and steel and contains a replica of the Australian outback and some of its more famous waterfalls. Inside this aviary-like structure, one can see birds flying freely about, a variety of turtles, and even a frill-necked lizard, *Chlamydosaurus kingii*. The frill-necked lizard, or "frilled dragon" in the pet trade, was made famous by the 1993 film *Jurassic Park*, in which the movie's *Dilopohosaurus wetherilli* sports an umbrella-like frill around its neck that it uses to intimidate predators (or human prey, in the film's case). In actuality, the dinosaur did not have this feature and it was simply borrowed for the story by Michael Crichton, the original novel's author, from the frill-necked lizard, in what some may call an act of artistic license. (An interesting theory [by me] posits that the dinosaurs featured in *Jurassic Park* have frills because the DNA of a frill-necked lizard was used to complete the gaps in the incomplete *Dilophosaurus* DNA, just as frogs were used, accounting for the twist that the animals can breed despite all being born female.)

The second building, known as the Pier 3 pavilion, is the largest, with five floors. It contains a majority of the exhibits and offices. The most prominent attraction is the Blacktip Reef exhibit. A 265,000-gallon pool of green water, guests can look down into this massive concrete tank to see a 500-pound green sea turtle, dozens of stingrays and sharks, and corals simulating an Indo-Pacific reef. A series of escalators leads visitors right over top of the reef, bringing them to various floors. The skeleton of a humpback whale hangs from the ceiling, looking much less like the gentle mammals we're used to seeing in movies and more like a great monster.

At the top of the Pier 3 pavilion is a glass pyramid known as the Upland Tropical Rainforest exhibit. Similar to the Australian exhibit, visitors can walk through a recreation of the Amazon jungle, complete with a low-hanging mist, waterfalls, and massive brown trees. Guests can check out the enormous fish that call the river home, a variety of monkeys, and even some bird-eating spiders (literally) that thankfully remain behind glass. At the end of the exhibit are also tanks of poison dart frogs. These colorful creatures, many of them no bigger than thumbnails, are deadly in the wild. They are known to secrete a lethal poison from their skin, which some tribal hunters have taken to coating on their arrows. (Hence the oft-used-but-inaccurate "poison arrow frog" name). However, they create the poison based off an alkaloid-rich diet in the wild, so captive specimens are not nearly as dangerous.

The third building, called the Pier 4 pavilion, houses the aquarium's dolphinarium. Opened in 1990, the dolphinarium is an absolutely enormous 1.3-million-gallon pool that houses eight Atlantic bottlenose dolphins, *Tursiops truncatus*. The pool is located beneath a glass ceiling, getting direct sunlight on cloudless days, and has been praised for its size and cleanliness by a number of organizations. Like any entity that keeps captive animals, it has of course come under fire. The Empty the Tanks movement has constantly put pressure on the National Aquarium to release its dolphins into the wild; the aquarium has reduced its dolphin "show" to make it less about entertainment and more about education, but at the time of writing the dolphins remain in captivity with no current plans to release them.

As well as the host of the gigantic dolphinarium, Pier 4 is also home to the aquarium's cafeteria where guests can buy overpriced slices of pizza and the gift shop where guests can buy overpriced stuffed animals. A life-size model of a humpback whale—complete with actual skin, unlike the one hanging over the Blacktip Reef exhibit—hovers over the cafeteria. There are a series of telescopes situated around the upper level of the cafeteria that allow guests to get a closer view of the whale model's more detailed features, like the strings of hair under its flippers or the barnacles around its eyes.

As fun and exciting as the many exhibits are, as mesmerized as I was by the institute's unequivocally vast menagerie, I was here for a very specific purpose: sharks.

Shark Alley, the National Aquarium's shark exhibit, may just be the most unique—and spookiest—in the world. Located in the Pier 3 pavilion, Shark Alley is a ring-shaped, 225,000-gallon aquarium that is over four stories tall. A spiraling ramp leads down the center of the ring, giving off the illusion that visitors are being encircled by the massive tank's monstrous inhabitants. It is dark. *Very* dark. There are mounted silhouettes of various shark species with dim LED lights softly glowing behind them, making them pop out. The water behind the thick glass appears almost black, the sandy bottom green and still, *very* still. There is no sound but the muffled, hesitant murmur of visitors, looking around with a mix of curiosity and fear as they move down the ramp. And then, from around the bend, a gigantic fish appears, its teeth beared. The car-sized monster swims by slowly, gracefully, only to have yet another swim by within moments to the "ooh"s and "ahh"s of the crowd.

Shark Alley's mysterious, dangerous atmosphere is unmistakable. The aquarium does a fantastic job of showing visitors the beauty of these large animals while simultaneously letting us feel the *danger* they present. Traversing the spiraling ramp is a tense experience, especially for those who may have already had reservations about going to the beach. It isn't uncommon to see young children bury their heads in their parents' chests until they reach the bottom and the world lights up again.

Shark Alley is home to a variety of large oceanic sharks. These include sand tiger sharks and sandbar sharks (*Carcharius taurus* and *Carcharhinus plumbeus* respectively), which look how most people would imagine traditional sharks; bulky, 8-foot-long bodies with brownish coloring and teeth like spikes. Nurse sharks, *Ginglymostoma cirratum*, are also prominently featured. These oddball sharks, while easily reaching 10 feet in length, have a flat body that skims along the bottom of its environment. Its mouth is oriented more like a stingray's in that it is smaller and designed to eat crustaceans it finds along the ocean floor.

The strangest, *biggest*, and most alien-looking of Shark Alley's residents, however, isn't a shark at all. Imagine a creature with the general body of a shark, including the dorsal fin and long caudal fins, only flatter, somewhere between a shark and a stingray. Nothing too spectacular; the nurse sharks have a similar body type, only significantly smaller. However, in the place of a nose, this animal has what looks like a *chainsaw* lying on its side, extending several feet in front of its face, rows of teeth protruding from it. This is called a rostrum, and it is what gives the largetooth sawfish, *Pristis pristis*, its otherworldly appearance.

As a child, I had spent countless hours walking up and down the ramp at Shark Alley, absolutely fascinated by it. It is like walking through another realm, an alien world full of monsters, where human beings are no longer the zenith of evolution. I so revered these animals that I was actually inspired to get a (regrettable) shark tattoo when I was 16, one I desperately wish I had a more romantic story for. So, after spending so much time peering through the glass into that dangerous, forbidden world, it was surreal to finally get behind it.

The grated metal catwalk I stood on was so close to the surface of the bubbling water that my shoes were getting wet. The salty odor of seawater is impossible to escape, reminding me of beach trips as a child. Concrete walls border each side of me. Rows of metal halide lights the size of basketball hoops point down into the water. A jumble of pipes runs along the ceiling a few feet over my head. There is a railing, but it looks rickety and unstable. Or at least it seems that way when I think about what lurks just below the surface.

I could barely hear Dr. Peter Bradford, the National Aquarium's Curator of Large Fish Exhibits, over the incessant mechanical chugging of the industrial-strength filtration systems I knew were lurking just behind the concrete walls. The sound was deafening in comparison to the other side of Shark Alley, where the eerie silence exacerbated the dreamlike atmosphere of isolation that made guests feel as if they were truly descending into the dark, cold depths of the abyss.

"The water is constantly filtered, so it's a little loud in here," Bradford said, smiling through his goatee. Below us, the surface was much more active than it looked from the spiraling catwalk. Water sprayed the walls, and the bottom of my pants, and Bradford's shiny head. It was difficult to make out any shapes, but occasionally I could see the intimidating silhouette of one of the aquarium's great fishes.

"How do you fill a tank like this?" I asked. "And is maintaining it any different from a smaller home aquarium? How did you build it?"

"Well, we filled it with water," Bradford answered with a smirk. He leaned against the railing of the catwalk and relaxed. I preferred to stay in the middle. Away from the water or any shaky railings. He continued, "Obviously we built everything first and then piped water in straight from the Chesapeake Bay. After that, we treated it and monitored all the levels until we knew it was right, then introduced test animals. Taking care of the water is basically the same as a small home aquarium, yes, but everything obviously needs to be bigger. Our filters are industrial strength and require daily maintenance; we have a whole department for it. Sharks, especially, are difficult to keep because their skin gives off ammonia and they're messy eaters, leading to even more spikes. These are some of the most powerful filters in the world, even though they work the same in principle as the small ones you can get at the pet store."

He went on to tell me that the National Aquarium was lucky in that it was situated on a harbor. The natural seawater they brought in to fill the Shark Alley tank needed only to be filtered and some salt added. Inland aquariums must take additional steps to fill their tanks. For example, the Georgia Aquarium in Atlanta filled their enormous Ocean Voyager exhibit with 6 *million* gallons of municipal tap water pumped in from the city. The aquarists then had to ship in 1.5 million pounds of synthetic sea salt and added it to the water until it had reached the desired levels.

"People have this tendency to think that sharks aren't as fragile as other, smaller animals," Bradford said. "But that isn't really the case. Just because an animal is bigger doesn't mean it's more resilient to environmental variances. One of the toughest animals on earth is the tardigrade, barely a millimeter long. [This is also known the water bear]. They can survive *outer space*. But take away oxygen from even the biggest land animal, let's say an elephant, and it'll die in minutes. The point is that sharks need to be treated just as carefully as any other aquarium fish."

"But do you have more leniencies with the shark tank?"

"Chemically? No. Everything has to stay consistent. Luckily, large aquariums such as this one are more chemically stable [as discussed earlier] but that doesn't mean we can go outside the typical environmental parameters. If one of these filters breaks, we have backups until it's fixed."

The pumping and filtration systems employed by the National Aquarium—and most public aquariums in general—are designed for incredible efficiency. "We almost never have to add water," Bradford told me. "The pumps are sealed so tight that evaporation isn't a concern. We don't use any more water than the average supermarket."

He went on to explain that the National Aquarium's water went through four treatment stages. First, the water is filtered mechanically by passing through fine meshes that remove larger particles. These meshes are constantly cleaned or swapped by the aquarium's marine Life Support Staff. In many aquariums, this mesh is actually comprised of sand surrounded by a nylon sheet, which traps various particles as the water passes through. The second phase is known as fractionation, which dissolves and removes harmful organic particles. The third and final stage is the addition of a chemical called ozone, which is similar to chlorine except safe for fish. Ozone is made up of three oxygen atoms, making it highly unstable and thus a perfect oxidizing agent. In the final stage, the filtered water is pumped into a holding tank with an open top, which allows any gasses that accumulated in the water throughout the treatment process to dissipate before it is pumped back into the exhibit.

"We have over two hundred pumps here at the National Aquarium, which are capable of filtering about two hundred thousand gallons per minute. Our goal is to keep the total water turnover in each exhibit at under two hours. [This means that all the water in the exhibit must be filtered in under two hours]. They need to run constantly. If they stop for even an hour, we could lose all of our fish."

"How are fish like these shipped?" I asked. "You can't exactly FedEx them."

"Actually," Bradford said, "you can, and most [public] aquariums do." He went on to explain how many of the animals, particularly the large sharks, are shipped via air by companies such as UPS. Specially-designed tanks are built that can circulate water, some of which can weigh up to 54,000 pounds or more for larger specimens. "One of the unique challenges you encounter with shipping sharks is that immobilization means death. Unlike a lot of other fish, they can't pump water through their gills without actually moving. They need their gills to extract oxygen from the water, so if they stop moving, they'll die. So the shipping tanks use special pumps to circulate water through their gills, and we have a full team of veterinarians travel with them and check on them constantly. Usually the air travel routes are planned out and we'll block off certain roads to make sure that the fish are transferred to the aquarium as quickly as possible once they're loaded into a truck on the ground."

"And once they're here, you just toss them in the tank?"

Bradford laughed. "Not at all. They need to be acclimated first. All large fish are put into a quarantine tank for a few weeks to make sure they're healthy enough to be released into the general population. They're also acclimated there."

Acclimation is the process by which a new fish is slowly introduced to water from their destination tank. Simply putting a fish into an established aquarium could shock it, since the water parameters of the tank may not match the water in which the animal was shipped. A sudden change in water quality can be devastating to the fish, causing unnecessary stress and even potentially killing it. Acclimation is achieved by keeping the fish in a quarantine tank, as described by Dr. Bradford, with water from the destination tank slowly added to the water in the shipping tank (while also taking out the same amount of water that was added). Eventually, the shipping tank will be full of water from the destination tank, but the gradual process by which this is done ensures that the animal's body will be able to gently adjust.

Keeping large animals in public aquariums, and going through all the obstacles required to not only get them there, acclimate them, and house them, isn't new. And it hasn't changed much. The first documented attempt to ship and house large marine animals was by none other than the famed P.T. Barnum in 1862. Barnum had six beluga whales, *Delphinapterus leucas*, shipped via boxcars loaded with moistened seaweed to New York. Accounts vary, but purportedly only one of the animals survived captivity for nearly two years. However, within a decade, beluga whales and other cetaceans were being shipped via train to aquariums all over the country—usually at a depressingly high mortality rate.

"So I assume that maintaining the filters is pretty much a constant job?" I asked.

"Yep. Oil changes, mesh changes, cleanings, seal inspections. It's constant." Once the artificial environments are "cured," as in the water is filtering and the parameters are met, the ecosystem pretty much remains stable. "These environments we create here are self-sustaining," Bradford explained. "As long as the filters don't stop pumping, everything should remain constant. We should never have to add or remove anything from the water or change it in any way. Regardless, we test it constantly."

Every day, the aquarium's staff collects water samples from each exhibit and runs them through various tests to ensure quality. Computers for each exhibit assist this process by measuring the water quality and providing charts to the staff, allowing them to make adjustments on the fly, if necessary.

"Once the animals are safe in their new homes, the real fun begins. Getting the animals acclimated is only half the battle. Taking care of them is a whole other story." The National Aquarium in Baltimore has a department dedicated solely to feeding the animals called the *husbandry commissary*. To the untrained eye, the commissary doesn't look any different than a restaurant kitchen. There are lines of chefs chopping up meats and prepping meals. "Our veterinarians assist our chefs with meal preparation for our facility's animals," Bradford said. "At any given moment, we've got something around twenty-five thousand pounds of food stored in our commissary. Everything is designed to provide the perfect nutritional balance for our animals. We don't just throw in some pet store fish flakes and call it a day. The USDA does random inspections, too, so we have to keep our kitchens sterile and clean."

Among the other facilities at the National Aquarium is an entire wing of laboratories that one could mistake for a human hospital. There are surgery centers, MRI machines, and an entire staff of vets wandering about in white lab coats. All of this, of course, is in the name of keeping every captive animal at the National Aquarium healthy and happy.

"So in this tank, Shark Alley, you've got some pretty big sharks," I said. "And they all seem pretty healthy, coming from someone who's not a vet and has really no idea what a healthy shark looks like as opposed to an unhealthy shark."

Bradford nodded.

"So why's it so hard to keep a Great White? Why have so many public aquariums failed? Obviously size isn't the issue…" Whale sharks are much larger than Great White sharks, and several aquariums around the world have managed to keep whale sharks with no issues.

"Well," he sighed, "there are a variety of reasons. One of the most obvious ones is that they're not peaceful animals. You're talking about one of the most aggressive, dangerous creatures on the planet. The insurance would be astronomical. This isn't a whale shark, which may be enormous but it's also so docile that you can ride on its back while it swims. This is a *Tyrannosaurus rex* in fish form." (side note: I loved his analogy so much that I actually used it for myself earlier in this piece, as you may have noticed. Don't judge me.)

He continued. "Just getting a Great White from the ocean and into an aquarium would be asking employees to put their lives at risk. And then once it's there, you have a whole host of new problems. For one thing, they're open ocean animals that have been known to swim hundreds of miles a week, so putting one in a relatively small aquarium is going to cause it so much stress that it'll freak out and start slamming against the side of the tank. It'll injure itself pretty easily. Once this happens, then they don't eat. It may be an animal that runs off instinct, but survival always comes before hunger. If it senses that it's trapped, and can't get away, eating is the last thing on its mind. If some kidnapper chains you up in a walk-in closet, will dinner be your first concern? No, and it won't be the Great White's, either. Most of the attempts to house these animals ended up with the sharks being released back into the wild almost immediately because getting them to eat in captivity is a monumental task compared to other, relatively docile sharks.

"And of course, with that aggression comes the fact that they can't share a tank. The whale sharks in Georgia and Japan can share aquariums with thousands of other fish because they're so peaceful. Even our sharks here aren't aggressive enough to attack each other. But Great Whites? That's a different story. You have to dedicate an entire exhibit just to them. They don't make good roommates."

From what Bradford explained, aggression was the primary reason that Great Whites were not very good captive animals. Size was irrelevant, but no aquarium would want to put up with the risk the sharks presented. Or at least that's the prevailing thought. As it turned out, the Great White is not alone in being difficult to keep in captivity.

"Believe it or not," Bradford said, "the shortfin mako shark is actually even harder to keep in captivity than a Great White." The shortfin mako, *Isurus oxyrinchus,* is one of the fastest fish in the world and, from what Bradford explained, does even worse in an aquarium than its much larger brethren. The longest surviving captive mako only lived for five days at the New Jersey Aquarium in 2001 before dying. Some of you may recall the cult 1999 film *Deep Blue Sea* (the one with Samuel L. Jackson), about an undersea lab that uses genetically-modified mako sharks—with rather predictable results for most horror films.

Keeping a Great White in captivity for a significant amount of time is, as Bradford was emphatic about, one of the most difficult tasks in the world given all of the circumstances and logistical hurdles surrounding the notorious monster fish. However, it was not impossible.

In fact, as you may be surprised to learn, it had actually been done before.

5
Jaws in Chains

eaLand's attempt to house a Great White, though by far the most infamous, was not the first. Several aquariums—though their plans nowhere near as ambitious—had at least toyed with the idea, and even sometimes experienced a modicum of success, of keeping these animals in captivity.

While the National Aquarium in Baltimore will always hold a special place in my heart, there is little doubt that the Monterey Bay Aquarium is superior in many ways. Located on a series of piers overlooking the Pacific Ocean in Monterey, California, the institution is at the zenith of aquarium technology and is frequently on the cutting edge of both exhibits and research. The aquarium, which from the outside looks no more spectacular than one of the many warehouses that surround it on Cannery Row, has played host to some of the most incredible feats in aquarium engineering the world has ever seen.

Opened in 1984, Monterey Bay Aquarium holds over 35,000 animals representing nearly 700 different species, many of whom make their home in the weird, wide, colorful Pacific Ocean; a gigantic, mostly-unexplored realm that takes up a third of the surface area on the *entire planet*. (And nearly *half* of earth's water). The facility hosts around 2 million annual visitors from all corners of the globe and is one of California's premier tourist attractions. It's been featured in film, scientific articles, and numerous documentaries. The institution even serves as a focal point for the 1986 film *Star Trek: The Voyage Home* (also known colloquially as "the one with the whales").

The Monterey Bay Aquarium is almost entirely privately funded. Construction of the aquarium tallied somewhere around $55 million, with much of that money coming in the form of a gift from David and Lucille Packard, the former of which is one of the founders of HP computers. Today, the facility is maintained by a few hundred employees and over a thousand seasonal volunteers, with guest admission covering most of its expenses.

The aquarium is known for its advances in research and works extensively with the Monterey Bay Aquarium Research Institute and the Center for Ocean Solutions. Even the water around the aquarium is protected; the facility is located within the Monterey Bay National Marine Sanctuary, the equivalent of a national park for a saltwater environment—complete with all the federal protections such a status offers. Children (and childlike adults) are also catered to, with the Monterey Bay Aquarium working in conjunction with Safari Ltd to produce scientifically accurate toys and figurines depicting various marine life.

One of the more impressive exhibits was founded on one of the more impressive firsts for aquariums: the kelp forest. Contained within a 28-foot-high, 330,000-gallon hexagonal aquarium, this undersea wonderland looks like something from a fairytale. Stalks of kelp grow like trees from the bottom, swaying gently in the artificial current as swarms of fish and small sharks swim amongst the foliage. It is truly like stepping into an underwater forest, a whimsical land of colorful, impossible creatures.

Kelp is fairly common along coastal waters and can grow upwards of 60 feet. A flexible green stem covered with thousands of leaves, kelp is actually a type of seaweed. Forests of this marine plant provide shelter for smaller fish and countless invertebrates, with some living their entire lives without ever leaving these undersea sanctuaries. These plants grow quickly, sometimes up to 10 inches *per day* under the right conditions, and can often be seen washing up on beaches.

However, as common as kelp is in the wild, it is difficult to house in captivity and the Monterey Bary Aquarium was the first to keep it successfully. It is the facility's unique location along the coast that allows this. The aquarium uses pumps to bring in water straight from Monterey Bay at a rate of nearly 2,000 gallons per *minute*. Water is constantly filtered, then pumped into the exhibits at a rate constant matching the current water from the exhibits being pumped *out* into the bay. This essentially makes the aquarium something of an artificial filter for its stretch of coast and, essentially, part of its ecology. What this does is allows for constant water movement and culture of microorganisms needed for kelp, which other aquariums lack. The top of the aquarium is also kept open, allowing maximum sunlight exposure.

As fascinating as kelp is (if you're sort of boring), I didn't travel across the country to learn about plants. I came to learn about fish. More to the point, a certain kind of fish.

The aquarium's Open Sea exhibit is one of the largest fish tanks in the world, rivaling the Georgia aquarium's massive display, at about 1.3 million gallons. It has hosted numerous large animals, including one of the world's only captive ocean sunfish, *Mola mola*. The ocean sunfish is the world's heaviest bony fish (sharks are much heavier but are cartilaginous, not bony) and looks like a flying disc, 14 feet across, with a wing at the bottom and a wing on top. The exhibit has also been the home of massive sardine schools, green sea turtles, blue tuna, moon jellies, and...Great White sharks.

The history of keeping Great White sharks in public aquariums—or at least the attempts to—is somewhat tragic. The first documented attempt was by the Marineland of the Pacific in 1955, which kept its Great White alive for a single day. Until 1981, the record for keeping one of these behemoths in captivity was *11 days*, held by a shark nicknamed Sandy, who lived briefly at the Steinhart Aquarium in San Francisco. This record was subsequently broken by SeaWorld San Diego in August of '81, who kept their specimen for...wait for it...16 days. The creature was released back into the wild after it became clear that it simply was not going to adapt to life as a captive. More recently, the Okinawa Churaumi Aquarium in Japan kept a Great White alive for only three days before it sank and died.

If any facility has had at least *some* success at keeping Great White sharks in captivity, it's the Monterey Bay Aquarium.

The aquarium's first attempt at housing a Great White came before it actually opened, and was an absolute failure.

The shark was slated to be the primary attraction on opening day, drawing visitors from around the world to witness the only captive Great White on the planet. Unfortunately, the animal died after about ten days, shortly before the aquarium opened to visitors for the first time.

However, nearly 20 years later, the institute would experience a (relatively) great success. A small female Great White, only about five feet long, was captured off the coast of Ventura, California, and was subsequently kept in the Monterey Bay Aquarium's Outer Bay exhibit for 198 days before she was released. The shark was thriving off a diet of salmon steaks and showed no signs of ill health. However, she also attacked two of her tank mates, a pair of soupfin sharks, *Galeorhinus galeus*, which both later died from their injuries.

In August 2006, the aquarium tried again. They introduced an even smaller specimen, a 5'8", 103-pound male, to their Outer Bay exhibit. This animal had been accidentally caught just outside Santa Monica Bay a few days earlier. Like the previous shark, his primary diet was composed of salmon steaks. After around 137 days in captivity, he was released after gaining over a foot in length and nearly 70 pounds, as it was deemed he'd be a danger to the tank's other inhabitants—not to mention to the veterinarians and other aquarium staff.

About a year later, Monterey Bay Aquarium housed a third Great White. This one was even smaller than the others, coming in at only about 4 and a half feet long and barely over 60 pounds—hardly threatening or logistically challenging. He survived for about 160 days before being released, again out of fear of him growing too large and dangerous for other specimens in the tank.

A fourth shark, a small female, was added in the summer of 2008. However, like so many captive Great Whites before her, she refused to eat and was released after only a few days. A fifth shark was exhibited for three months in the fall of 2009, but tracking data indicated that she had been killed shortly after her release, getting caught in some netting off the coast of Ensenada in Mexico. A sixth shark, also less than five feet long, was housed for three months starting in August 2011 before its release.

The relative success of the Monterey Bay Aquarium may perplex some readers. How can it be called "success" when every specimen was borderline tiny and was only kept for a few months? The answer is simple: in the grand scheme of keeping Great Whites in captivity, those *are* relatively monumental successes. Obviously the standard isn't very high.

That's what makes what SeaLand attempted in 2015 such an interesting story. The Monterey Bay Aquarium captured and housed its collection of various Great Whites with the intention of keeping them only temporarily. SeaLand intended to keep their shark, Brody, as a permanent fixture. Like Icarus, their wings would also melt.

"What are some of the challenges you faced when keeping the Great Whites?" I asked en employee of the Monterey Bay Aquarium, who did not sign release forms and thus their name cannot be used.

"The biggest problem is acclimation," they told me. "They can't just be dumped into the aquarium, but they're also too big—even the small ones—to put in quarantine housing. We have to make sure they're healthy and swimming properly, especially with the specimens who are caught by fishermen." It was explained that the sharks were first kept in an open ocean holding pen off the coast of Malibu. These pens are essentially steel wire pens that can be opened to allow the sharks to swim free if the staff detects any issues. The sharks are observed for several weeks before being transported to the aquarium's exhibits.

"The first shark in 2004, why was it so successful compared to the others?" I asked. "And why did it attack the other two sharks? Were you expecting that?"

"The first shark was well fed and typically not aggressive. Our suspicion is that she only attacked the other two sharks to defend her perceived territory. She didn't actually eat the soupfin sharks, just bit them. They bled out later. To be honest, we were planning on releasing her soon anyway, so the attack just sort of kicked us in the right direction. She was getting too big for the tank. That's one of the most obvious challenges of keeping Great Whites. They're big and aggressive. Whale sharks are bigger, sure, but they're peaceful. We thought it was best to release her before she got too big and difficult to move."

"And the sharks are all tagged once they're released?"

"Oh yes. The end goal of the aquarium is research. Every large animal we release is tagged, and we can track it all over the globe." Great White sharks in particular are known for travelling vast distances, accounting for one of the many reasons they're so difficult to keep in captivity. It isn't uncommon for them to swim all the way across an ocean in just a few short months, or even weeks.

"What about feeding? These are hunters, right? How can you get them to eat in captivity?"

"I would describe them more as 'opportunistic' feeders," the employee clarified. "Yes, they're hunters in one sense. But they won't typically pass up any food. It's not uncommon to see them ripping off chunks of a floating whale carcass or even attacking lobster traps."

"What do you feed them here?"

"Salmon or tuna, typically. We have feeding shows." The Monterey Bay Aquarium actually airs their feeding shows live over the internet. While it's been over half a decade (at the time of this writing) since they housed a Great White, you can still see old clips all over the internet of the sharks ripping chunks of salmon and/or tuna from a dangling wire. "Getting them to eat is the hardest part of the process. It's why so many that are taken into captivity either die or have to be released within a few days. It's always a sort of '*Thank God!*' moment whenever one of them finally takes a bite of something that isn't one of its tank mates."

"You'd never consider feeding them seals, like in the wild?"

"Absolutely not. Yes, that happens in nature and seals are one of the Great White's primary food sources, but that's not something we can get away with here. Especially from a PR standpoint. Seals are cute and cuddly. We have them here on display. Salmon and tuna are things humans eat, too, so there's no issue there."

"And once the shark is eating and swimming around, what other problems do you face? That are unique to sharks, anyway."

"Hitting the walls is a huge issue," the employee explained. "Even the one we had here for over six months had injuries to her nose because she kept hitting the glass walls of the tank."

"Is their vision bad? Seems like they can see pretty well."
I told the employee how I'd witnessed the sharks feeding on
seals off Cape Town. Their movements, at that time, seemed
swift and precise; movement that could only be
accomplished with excellent vision.

"No, their vision's fine. The problem is electroreception."

If you were to get uncomfortably close to a shark's head,
you might notice (if you are not busy swimming for your
life) that its snout is lined with a number of black pores of
varying sizes, looking very much spots of mold in a frat
house bathtub. Inside these pores are small cells filled with
electrically-conductive jelly known as the ampullae of
Lorenzini, named for the 17th-century scientist. Laymen like
me simply call them electroreceptors.

"Sharks use these ampullae to detect electric fields in the
water," the employee said. "They're actually the most
electrically sensitive animals in the world. They can detect
something like five billionths of a volt."

"And what do they use this for?"

"To track prey. All animals, including their prey, give off
electrical signals. So sharks can find prey buried in the sand,
or in murky water. Virtually any living thing gives off a tiny
electrical signal. And not just living things…"

Glass, as the employee told me, also gives off a small
electrical charge. In fact, it's this mechanism that allows
modern touch screens to work so efficiently. The glass of
your smartphone produces a small electric field that is
interrupted when you press your finger to it. The phone's
computer reads the location of this interruption and
interprets it as a button press.

"The glass in an aquarium, we think anyway, can mess with the Great Whites sense of electroreception and cause it to bump into the walls. Very often when aquariums try to house them, they have to release them so quickly just to keep them from hurting themselves."

Despite the numerous challenges that keeping Great Whites presented, the Monterey Bay Aquarium had at least proven that it was possible—if only for a short time and with tiny, juvenile specimens. What SeaLand had attempted the previous summer was far more ambitious, however. The employee assured me that no other aquarium in the world would have seriously considered it, especially with an animal as large as Brody.

But they tried. And it all started with one of the most intense animal captures in history.

6
Catch and Release

It was a day or two after Tropical Storm Ana had dissipated that Dr. Anna Harding and James Warren met in a small conference room at SeaLand. Their discussion revolved around the 16-foot Great White shark that was currently wandering aimlessly around Murrell's Inlet, drawing crowds of onlookers and biting docked boats.

Anna Harding is 32 but looks 22. Standing barely over five feet tall and weighing maybe a little over 100 pounds, Dr. Harding surely doesn't fit the image of the macho, stereotypical animal wrangler seen in movies and TV shows. Her short, platinum blond hair, plentiful tattoos, and summery, smiley demeanor certainly didn't help matters. Picturing a squabble between her and James Warren—a tall, imposing African American man much older and larger than her—made me chuckle a bit. But Harding is tenacious, aggressive, intelligent, and incredibly well-respected, and her arguments admittedly gave me pause for thought.

"I was completely against the decision to bring in Brody," she said emphatically as we started our second round of drinks so fruity that I could feel my chest hair falling off. "I wanted to get him out of the inlet and release him a few miles offshore. James [Warren] told me he was planning on bringing in the shark and I flipped. Don't get me wrong, I love challenges and I love Great Whites, but this wasn't what we needed."

"That surprises me," I said, surprised. "I figured a scientist like you would love the idea of getting to work with a Great White."

"A small one, sure," she replied. "The Monterey Bay Aquarium houses sharks that were about five feet long. Brody was *sixteen* feet! That's a giant, deadly animal that has no place being in captivity. Trust me, I was thinking as much for my safety and the park's visitors' safety as much as Brody's. Guess in the end, I was right." She ended that statement with an audible sigh.

While in the grand scheme of history, zoos have been relatively safe for both guests, employees and animals, there are a number of infamous instances where that was simply not the case. There have been several fatalities—and even more near-misses—since the inception of these unique parks.

In 1996, a 24-year-old caretaker was attacked by five gray wolves at a wildlife preserve in Ontario, Canada. Up until that point, the wolves had been shy animals who stayed away from humans who'd entered their enclosure. Her body was torn to pieces. In 2012, Mila, an African elephant, killed the owner of the Franklin Zoo by crushing her with her trunk. Mila had been at the zoo for a number of years and was considered a peaceful resident.

Fatalities have not been restricted to zoo staff. Guests have also been killed. In 2012, a toddler fell over the railing of the Pittsburgh Zoo's painted dog exhibit (similar to hyenas). Autopsy results indicated that he survived the fall but was killed by the dogs, who tore the child to shreds. Even cute, cuddly animals like tapirs—who look like mini pig and elephant hybrids—have been documented to attack their keepers, in one case even ripping off the arm of zookeeper Lisa Morehead during a routine feeding gone wrong.

"There have been so many accidents involving non-aggressive animals," Harding said. "So now we're going to introduce one that is *known* for its aggression? Crazy."

"So how did the argument go?" I asked.

She shrugged. "James brought up all the conservation efforts that could come from it. Putting an animal like this on display. He did mention the profits, which pissed me off, but he wasn't wrong." SeaWorld's Great White in 1981 attracted nearly 40,000 visitors over a few days. Myrtle Beach's SeaLand was lucky to get that many visitors a month. "The money could be used to fund conservation efforts and raise awareness. And knowing James, most of it would be. I hate the fact that he's also an accountant, but I can't deny that he loves the ocean. It's just that he's willing to sacrifice certain values for that protection and I'm not. Most of the time, anyway. He sees things as a means to an end, I think it's possible to get to that end while avoiding those things. Does that make sense?"

It did, in a way. I got the feeling that Harding and Warren's relationship wasn't as antagonistic as the papers had made it seem in the days and weeks after the titular incident of this work. If anything, I could feel the respect for the man in her words, and got the same impression from James Warren when he spoke of Anna Harding.

"Look, I get the whole conservation thing. I see all the

good keeping the shark could do, I really do. But I was just cautious. I didn't want another Tire Reef on our hands," she said.

The term "Tire Reef" is a reference to any well-intentioned plan to protect the environment that backfires disastrously. I'll admit I hadn't heard it before speaking to Dr. Harding, so I imagined it was only an idiom thrown around in naturalist circles, a fraternity to which I hadn't belonged. The history of the term is nothing short of fascinating, and a poignant metaphor for the often destructive trap that is mankind's monumental ambitions.

In 1972, the construction of an artificial reef off the coast of Ft. Lauderdale, Florida was proposed by Broward Artificial Reef, Inc. The reef, known as Osborne Reef, would use thousands upon thousands of old rubber tires. The idea was that marine life such as corals, fish, and other invertebrates would use the tires as homes, which would in turn attract and increase the number of game fish in the area. Artificial reefs, constructed from varying materials, are not a new concept. They were first used by the ancient Persians to block the mouth of the Tigris River and keep out pirates. Even the Romans built them during the First Punic War to trap enemy ships. In the 1800s, fishermen off the coast of South Carolina used spare logs from cabins to build artificial reefs and attract more fish; the remnants of many can still be seen today. In modernity, many things are used for making reefs, including old refrigerators, old tanks, and even subway trains. Any sunken ship, given it's in water shallow enough for light to penetrate, will become a reef if not salvaged.

But tires…tires were a different story.

The project was so lauded that Goodyear dropped a golden tire from a blimp into the future reef site to christen it. Hundreds of private boats and the USS *Thrush* helped dump approximately two *million* old tires into the ocean, at a depth of around 65 feet, about a mile offshore. The reef covered an enormous area of 36 acres, and was initially celebrated as a rousing success.

But then...

The genius engineers, with their years of planning the Osborne Reef project, forgot one crucial element: tires are light, and ocean water moves.

Originally, the tires had been fastened together with nylon sheets and steel clips to prevent them from moving. A bunch of weights bound together are much more stable than on their own. However, those in charge of the project didn't account for the water's corrosivity toward the steel, and the majority of the clips failed. This resulted in the tires being strewn about in the currents, making it impossible for any marine life to attach to them. Some tires even swept so far from the reef that they *destroyed* other natural reefs! Many even began washing up on beaches and destroying local ecosystems.

In 2001, the first cleanup efforts began on a grant from the National Oceanic and Atmospheric Administration, but only 1,600 tires were initially removed. Between 2007 and 2009, even the US military got involved in the removal of the tires—which were now spread out over hundreds of miles and causing irreparable environmental damage. However, to date, fewer than 100,000 of the 2 million tires that were dumped have been recovered, costing hundreds of thousands of dollars.

Osborne Reef represents the nadir of conservation failure, good intentions gone astray. Nearly 50 years after the reef's construction, the ecological impacts are still devastating the local systems and will continue to do so for decades into the future.

"James had good intentions," Dr. Harding said. "But all I could think about were the potential ramifications. I'm a biologist. I work with whales and dolphins and sharks. There isn't anything I want more than to protect them, but I know where the line is. James didn't. James respected the idea, but he didn't respect the animal. And that's why we're here right now."

"So why did you end up working with Brody if you were so against it?" I asked. A part of me knew the answer already. We've all done dumb things because that dumb thing also happened to be a *once-in-a-lifetime* dumb thing.

"James wasn't going to back down," she insisted. "The decision had been made. They were already filling Darcy's old pool." SeaLand's old killer whale pool would serve as Brody's home. While the recovery operation of the shark was taking place, Warren was having it filled with seawater straight from the Atlantic Ocean with help from the local fire department. They'd literally pump water into some free trucks, drive to SeaLand, and spit the water back out. Using natural seawater would assist with Brody's acclimation.

"So you decided to just go with it anyway?"

"In a nutshell, yes. I guess you could say that it wasn't really much of a debate, or him asking for my thoughts. He was just telling me that it was going to happen, whether I liked it or not. So I decided that if they were going to do this no matter what, then I might as well have gotten involved.

Not every day you get to work with a Great White, especially one so big."

"Once in a lifetime," I chuckled.

"I did make some demands, though." She went on to explain that all staff access to Brody had to go through her. She would be in charge. And if she deemed, after a any length of time, that Brody was not fit for life in an aquarium and that his health was at risk, then Warren would agree to release him. "I made it very clear, that if I felt that this animal was in danger from being in captivity, that James had to abide by my recommendation."

"Then it's not a recommendation. It's an order."

"Call it what you want. We discussed it. Call it a gentleman's agreement. If I felt Brody was suffering, I'd write up a report with all my evidence and present it to him. If he didn't take my advice, then I'd present it to the USDA."

Her last request to Warren was for the expansion of the zoo's Emergency Response Team (ERT). These teams are essentially glorified animal control officers that are employed to restrain and capture any animals that may escape their enclosures, with particular emphasis put on ones that might be a danger to visitors. Many larger zoos employed entire squads that used equipment such as pepper sprays, tasers, tranquilizer guns, and even standard firearms for the especially dangerous exhibits. Most emergency response teams at US zoos used colors to indicate threat levels. Code Yellow was used for when a non-threatening animal, such as a parrot or a turtle, escaped. Code Blue is for large but peaceful animals that could cause accidental injury, like giraffes and zebras. Finally, Code Red is used when a dangerous animal such as a lion, tiger or crocodile escapes.

At that time, SeaLand employed two people on its emergency response team, and they were almost exclusively used as first aid workers to treat kids who decided to squeeze a sea urchin too hard in a touch tank or tripped going up some stairs.

Anna Harding was adamant about having an entire team *just* for Brody. The shark would be the most dangerous animal that SeaLand had ever kept. She wanted a team of at least three on hand at all times, and she wanted them to have weapons, something their current ERT workers didn't have.

"It was a ridiculous request," James Warren would tell me sometime later. "This isn't a lion or tiger that can get out and roam around and attack visitors. This was a fish. I get that it's some iconic, legendary animal with this mystique, but at the end of the day it's still a big fish that lives in a self-contained world. It's not going to grow legs, jump out of the tank, and run around eating visitors."

However, out of respect for his employee, colleague, and friend, Warren did in fact contract three new employees for SeaLand's ERT.

And, unbeknownst to him at the time, they'd indeed come in handy.

Catching a Great White shark unharmed, especially one as large as Brody, is obviously not a simple operation. It took the combined efforts of over one hundred people gathered along the banks of Murrell's Inlet days after Tropical Storm Ana to get the job done, and even so there were a few hurdles. More than once, James Warren, who supervised the transport, doubted whether it was possible.

"I can't tell you how many hours I spent on the phone talking to Myrtle Beach officials to try and get them to delay the excavation of the inlet's mouth for a few days," Warren said. "We went door-to-door to the locals asking for patience. They weren't happy with a sixteen-foot shark roaming around their docks. One guy threatened to shoot it. Nice guy."

Television news crews descended upon the inlet to record the capture of Brody, the giant shark. Most were disappointed, from what I understand, that the fish didn't invoke the monstrous image they were expecting.

"He basically just swam around slowly, confused," Warren told me. "He didn't even show any interest in our boats." SeaLand had dispatched several rafts into the main creek of the inlet to follow Brody, day and night, as his tank was being prepared and the procedures for his transfer were being finalized. Anna Harding was on one of the boats and was in charge of keeping track of the shark.

"We had people running routes from the inlet back to the park with stop watches," Warren explained. "The city had refused to shut down any roads for us, so we had to make due with the routes available." For the better part of a day, employees of SeaLand would drive back and forth between the park and the inlet and time the results according to different routes at different times of the day. "We averaged about a half hour, but by taking a route that allowed for more right turns than left turns, we were able to cut it by a few minutes. Every second counted."

Once the route was decided, the transport container was moved to the inlet and placed along the water near a cove.

The container looked no different than a standard shipping container with an open top. Inside was seawater from the inlet and two pumps on either side. The pumps circulated the water throughout the container, allowing it to pass through the shark's gills.

"Still water means death to a shark," Warren said. "The pumps keep the water flowing, as well as the oxygen. You can't just put a shark in a tank of still water like you can most other fish unless it can move around because their gills need circulation to extract oxygen. So, with that in mind, we have special transport tanks built just for sharks. They're a lot heavier than most because of all the extra machinery, but it's been proven they work. The Georgia Aquarium flew their whale sharks all the way from Taiwan using these tanks. Once they're filled with water and the animals, they can weigh about twenty-five tons or so."

Shipping animals is tricky business, as every animal has special requirements for survival. A good rule that many animal shippers use, despite the inevitable protests from animal rights groups, is the smaller and darker the shipping container, the better. A smaller container, with less room to move about, means less chance of an animal hurting itself during transport. Fish are often shipped in plastic bags of oxygen. Reptiles can be shipped in nylon sacks or even little plastic containers. Siamese fighting fish, because they require very little water to survive and cannot interact with each other, are often shipped in baggies no bigger than ketchup packets! One other common denominator is that they're all shipped in the dark, which reduces stress; what an animal can't see, it can't worry about.

On the day of the move, SeaLand brought in an animal

transport crane and placed it next to the shipping container, which was itself on a large truck bed that would be driven to the park, where staff was eagerly—and nervously—awaiting Brody's arrival. The crane held a thick nylon tarp capable of holding several thousand pounds, held to the crane's jib by steel cables. At about 6 o' clock in the morning, the operation commenced. They started early to ensure they'd have the entire day to make the capture and account for any unforeseen difficulties. The crane operator began by lowering the tarp into the water, where it flattened out. Now, all the SeaLand staff had to do was corral Brody into the tarp.

"Brody was not cooperative, to say the least," Anna Harding remembered. "We started out with chum to try and lure him into the area of the tarp. Didn't work. I think our boats agitated him."

Chumming is a colloquial term for using a medley of fish parts, blood, bone, and other fleshy guts as a lure to attract fish and, most notably, sharks. This mixture is known, simply enough, as chum. You may recall one of the more famous scenes from the 1975 film *Jaws* where Roy Scheider is seen flipping buckets of fish guts into the water shortly before the titular giant shark makes its first on-screen appearance. (This is the "bigger boat" scene). Chumming is typically very effective, but also sometimes frowned upon, as there are (unsubstantiated) claims that it teaches sharks to associate the presence of humans with being fed.

"It started getting dark when we decided we needed to take more drastic measures," Dr. Harding said. "The news crews were leaving, which was fine with us. And mosquitoes are most active at dusk, so they started driving away the spectators, which was also good. So without a lot of people looking, we bent the ethical rules just a little bit." Anna described their actions as "harsh to those who don't know any better." In other words, any keyboard warrior with a Twitter account would have condemned what the SeaLand staff did to get Brody into the tarp, even if in practice it barely harmed the shark at all.

"We got as close as we could and slapped him, hoping to scare him into the tarp." A shark's skin is like armor. A bullet would have trouble piercing the hide of a Great White. But even so, even the very implication that they could have possibly harmed the shark would be enough to send the idiotic internet outrage machine into a feeding frenzy (pun intended), so SeaLand embraced the cover of darkness and, around 9 o' clock in the evening, finally got Brody to swim into the tarp.

What followed was a frightening scene that made James Warren sweat more than the brutal heat and humidity of that muggy afternoon.

"We gave the signal for the crane operator to pull up and the tarp lifted out of the water with the shark," James Warren recalled. "At first it was beautiful. The tarp formed around the shark like a taco shell. The animal was probably confused at first, but it wasn't being harmed. It was smooth sailing until it started thrashing around." Warren described the tense scene wherein Brody began thrashing about much akin to any smaller fish you've seen flopping around on a dock, only exponentially more violent. "You're talking about a six thousand-pound animal fighting with all its might. I swore I could see the wheels of the crane come off the ground. When we swung the shark over the transport tank, we had to wait for it to calm down. If we'd lowered it in while it was flipping around, we it could've seriously hurt itself. It took, oh, I don't know, maybe five minutes before it finally settled down. By that time most of the crew had come ashore and were on the truck bed. When we finally lowered the tarp into the tank, we had to unhook one side of it from the crane."

One of the staffers had climbed to the top of the transport container and started detaching the tarp from the crane when Brody, undoubtedly in fright, slammed into the side of the container and knocked the staffer into the water.

"I almost threw up," Warren said. "I had my first second thought at that moment, when I saw the kid fall into the container with the shark."

Luckily, the container was not wide enough for Brody to actually turn around, and though the staffer got to experience the crushing *smack* of the fish's tail, he otherwise climbed out unharmed.

"I gave James [Warren] a hell of a look," Dr. Anna Harding would tell me alter. "As soon as he climbed out, I gave him 'I told you this was a bad idea' look. I think he got the message."

"I remember that look Anna gave me," Warren told me when I asked him about it. "I'll always remember it," he smirked. "I'm probably going to remember it every time I'm about to make a dumb decision for the rest of my life."

Once Brody was safely in the transport container and the tarp detached and hooked to the side, Anna Harding and a few other staffers did a final inspection to ensure that the life support system—the pumps circulating water through the container—were functioning properly. Warren, from what I understand, had grown impatient after a few minutes and wanted to get the animal to the park immediately. Dr. Harding finally gave the all-clear and a separate tarp was stretched over the top of the container and anchored to the truck bed.

"We didn't have a police escort. They were too busy helping clean up the other messes the tropical storm left behind." Warren didn't sound happy about that fact, but he didn't sound spiteful, either. I got the feeling he understood that transporting a shark was probably low on Myrtle Beach's priority list. "Luckily traffic wasn't terrible. Anna [Harding] rode with the shark. We got to the park in twenty-five or so minutes, if I recall. The inspection took ten minutes, plus the five or so for it to calm down. All in all, it'd been out of the water for almost forty minutes and I was nervous."

The moment of truth came shortly after Brody arrived at SeaLand. The truck maneuvered carefully through the park until it had reached Darcy's old pool, where another crane was waiting.

"We just did the same thing in reverse when we got there," Warren said. "We hooked the tarp back up to the crane and lifted him up." When Brody was placed in the pool, he slithered out of the tarp with a burst of speed—then immediately smacked into a wall.

"I gave James [Warren] another look," Anna told me with a sly grin. "I was almost ready to tell him we needed to take this thing back to the ocean. But then he calmed down and started swimming around slowly, checking things out. It was relieving."

The transport had been successful. Myrtle Beach

authorities started working on excavating the sand and gravel closing the mouth of Murrell's Inlet while the staff of SeaLand basked in a spell of cautious optimism. However, that was only the start. The tank had been set up for a killer whale, not a Great White shark—or any fish, really. And now that Brody was in place, the real work could begin.

"The easy part was over," James Warren said.

I asked, "That part was easy?"

"In comparison to what came next? Yeah. Real easy."

7
Just Keep Swimming

For the first few days of Brody's captivity, Dr. Anna Harding survived off a diet of energy drinks and gas station burritos filled with mushy egg and bit of meat that was advertised as bacon but not quite bacon, slathered in some sort of artificial cheese product trying to pass as cheddar. "I've never been a parent, but I've heard a lot of horror stories of those first few weeks after having a new baby, especially your first baby," she told me. "Sleepless nights, constant anxiety…I didn't see my apartment at all for a week."

"What kind of problems did you run into?" I asked.

"Well, the garden variety, of course. He kept hitting the side of the pool, so he'd scrape his face constantly. Great Whites, as you know by now, are open ocean predators. They're not used to being confined."

The pool at SeaLand, which was now dubbed the Domain of the King by the park's marketing department, is a near-perfect circle exactly 60 feet in diameter and 14 feet deep, with no slope. Most of the pool is underground, with a subterranean viewing area beneath for visitors, with the top 7 feet made up of a rim of thick acrylic. For the moment, SeaLand had left about 4 feet of space between the top of the rim and the waterline, making the total depth about 10 feet and bringing the total volume of the pool to 211,000 gallons. When Brody was first introduced to the pool, it was completely bare; white concrete floors and walls with no décor to speak of.

"We kept the water level away from the edge of the pool to minimize the risk of Brody somehow flopping out," Anna said. "James [Warren] already had contractors at the site putting plans together for adding wire bars at the top and a roof to keep out rain." The wire bars Anna had referred to would extend a few feet from the rim of the pool toward the center. This would ensure that there was no way Brody could make a daring escape into the grandstands that surrounded the pool. While the roof was never finished before the accident, the plan was to make it an air-supported tent that would keep out rain and any debris frequent storms may have carried.

I asked, "Would rain have really been that big of a deal? I mean, it rains on the ocean…"

"Yes, but the ocean is a much larger body of water, obviously, and is more stable. Brody's pool was big enough to where it probably wasn't going to make a huge difference, especially since all the water in the tank was filtered every two hours, but James wanted to be safe."

I'd learn later that the proposed roof would also serve another function: darkness. Later, we will discuss Warren's efforts to market the shark, and keeping the exhibit dark and spooky was one of the ideas.

"I kept track of Brody like crazy those first few days," Anna said. "I never left the exhibit. When I needed to rest, I'd sleep in the control room."

The pool's control room looked like a tiny version of mission control. It's a little office overlooking the pool, filled with computer monitors displaying graphs and charts of the current levels such as salinity and temperature. There are also several screens showing video feeds from inside the pool, where numerous little cameras are placed. One can flip through the screens to see footage of the pump station dedicated to the pool, located in a maintenance area below ground, and the exterior of the pool. Keeping constant watch on the animals and the guests is the utmost priority of any zoo. At any moment, a kid could throw something into an exhibit—or fall into one—and zoos and aquariums must be prepared to handle said situations at a second's notice.

"After a few days, he stopped running into the walls. Or at least didn't do it as much," Anna recalled. "It was a pretty glorious moment when I saw him about to ram into the side of the pool but then make a sharp turn and head back toward the middle."

Once a week had passed and Brody appeared to be at least tolerating his surroundings, SeaLand had decided it was time for an initial medical checkup.

"How in the hell do you do a checkup on a shark? Especially one that big?"

"Wasn't easy," Anna said. "At first we tried to draw him over to the work island so we could get a closer look." The work island in Brody's pool was a small floating platform about 10 feet in diameter. It was used by trainers and vets to perform routine medical checks of Darcy the killer whale and was tethered to the side of the tank. Before using it to check on Brody, Anna had insisted that steel railings be set along the circumference of the work island. Warren didn't hesitate to agree.

"We couldn't really get a good look at him from the island, and he wasn't exactly keen on coming close enough for us to, anyway. We had to come up with another solution."

In most aquariums, divers typically have no problem getting in the water with their pelagic sharks. Whether it's the Monterey Bay Aquarium, the National Aquarium, or smaller zoological parks such as the South Carolina Aquarium, the sharks are never dangerous enough to not get in the water with them.

Even outside aquaria, shark diving is a popular tourist activity for those brave enough (and rich enough to afford it). These tourists, and those working in aquariums housing pelagic sharks, wear special suits made of chainmail, uncreatively called shark suits. However, even a suit of armor is no match for a large Great White shark, so SeaLand had to resort to other means of getting in the water with Brody.

Shark cages have been around since the early 1970s and are believed to have originated when oyster divers needed a means to reach the seafloor without being attacked by sharks. They're typically made of steel and float near the surface using buoys. Their tops are usually open, allowing observers to easily climb in and out. They may be used by people in scuba gear or snorkels, and allow those inside to get up close and personal with large, dangerous sharks. Today, shark cages are used primarily for two purposes: research and tourism.

Shark cage tourism is on par with shark diving in popularity, and possibly even more so since it does not technically *require* users to be experienced divers. Those paying for the experience need only a swimsuit to enjoy seeing sharks up close behind the safety of the steel bars. However, the popularity of shark cage tourism has also given rise to the controversial practice of shark baiting, wherein tour guides purposely drop chum into the water in order to attract schools of dangerous sharks.

This activity creates two issues and was actually banned by the state of Florida in 2001. Firstly, as stated earlier in this piece, baiting sharks teaches them to associate humans with food. This, like Pavlov's famous dog, makes human presence akin to a dinner bell. The second problem is collateral damage: drawing masses of sharks to a single area could have a detrimental effect on anything outside the protective shark cage. In 2008, a tour guide in the Bahamas baited a number of sharks for a group of tourists, some of which were not in a cage. One of these tourists, 49-year-old Markus Groh, died of blood loss when he was bitten by a shark of undocumented species that had been agitated by the crates of bait.

"We used a shark cage to get in the water with Brody," Dr. Harding said. "We actually had to go pick one up from a local tourist trap. We didn't have one on hand." SeaLand, and in fact most aquariums, did not need such devices, as most of the sharks kept in public aquaria are large but not big enough to be undeterred by shark suits. Brody was a different story. "So the first day, me and a dive specialist are in the cage, and Brody stays as far away from it as he can. He starts circling us along the edge of the pool. We managed to lure him in closer with a slab of tuna, but he slammed into the bars and bit down. The buoys started to sink and I almost lost my lunch. It was terrifying. He left us alone after that and the buoys held, but man, that moment...I can't even describe it. Here's this giant animal that can literally bite your head off, and I got to stare down its throat for a split second. I'll never forget it."

Shark cages are not perfect. They have failed in the past and will fail again by the time this work goes from the printer to your hands. And they almost always involve Great White sharks.

In 2005, an enormous Great White measuring nearly 20 feet in length managed to bite through the bars of a recreational shark cage off the coast of South Africa. The captain of the boat had attempted to fend off the shark using whatever he had on board, but it was to no avail, as the Great White had determined two things: it wanted the human inside the cage and it was not going to give up. The shark bit through the buoys keeping the cage afloat and it slowly started to sink.

And the tourist inside was not wearing scuba gear.

Like something from a horror movie, the tourist realized one of two things were probably going to happen: he was going to drown if he stayed in the cage, or possibly get eaten if he made a break for it. Luck was on his side, as he managed to get to the boat before the shark got to him, but the incident still served as a chilling example of the consequences of turning nature into a tourist attraction and the danger of shark diving.

"Did you stay in the water?" I asked Anna.

"Yes, I had to inspect him after all."

"You really felt in danger? Didn't sense any sort of bond with Brody? Seems like you'd been motherly up till then."

"You really think that matters?" She laughed. "Look, I get it. People have this ingrained desire to humanize animals, and that's fine, especially if it leads to respect for them. But just because you're compassionate for them doesn't mean that they're compassionate for you. People either don't know that, or choose not to believe it. I love animals, I respect animals, but they're still *animals*, driven by instinct and the will to survive, and they'll defend themselves, violently if need be, if they feel threatened. My 'bond' with Brody doesn't mean anything. I'm still a piece of meat to him. People want so badly to believe that animals have the same sense of compassion they do, and that's just not the case, that's *not* reality, and every real expert knows that. *That's* why we have to respect them as much as we do. We could all be the next Dawn Brancheau at any moment, especially when working with dangerous creatures."

Dawn Brancheau was one of the three people killed by the orca known as Tilikum, a mainstay at SeaWorld parks for decades. Brancheau had been working with the orcas for 14 years and had developed quite a bond with Tilikum, the largest resident whale. However, Brancheau tragically met her end at the mouth of the same creatures she had dedicated her life to protecting. On February 24, 2010, Brancheau was pulled into the water by Tilikum during a routine show and was drowned by the massive animal, which simply refused to let her go. The SeaWorld staff did everything they could to get the animal to release her, but it was all for naught, as by the time the orca finally let go, the star trainer was long deceased, her body battered beyond recognition.

The incident rocked the world. SeaWorld immediately

forbade any trainers from getting in the water with the whales, which was followed up by a direct ban on the practice by the Occupational Safety and Health Administration. Animal rights groups used the accident to propagate their political agendas, and given that the death of a human being was involved, it was pretty much impossible to refute their points without being posited as a monster. The documentary *Blackfish* came out some years later, only engendering the public's newfound hesitance to accept the idea of keeping killer whales in captivity.

The death of Dawn Brancheau, and SeaWorld's failure to save the poor woman from the jaws of death, can be compared to a more recent incident. Both of these accidents, which occurred at zoos, led to an onslaught of public outrage, even though both had ***exact opposite*** outcomes, which leads credence to the idea that internet mobs don't care about the actual event and more about believing that they're on some sort of moral high ground above everyone else. I'm speaking, of course, of the Harambe incident.

If there is one case that so beautifully demonstrates American moral hypocrisy and our innate need to act as a judge, jury, and executioner despite having very little if any knowledge of the facts, it's the incident that occurred at the Cincinnati Zoo on May 28, 2016. A three-year-old child escaped the eyes of his mother for a few seconds and managed to climb the fence of the zoo's silverback gorilla enclosure. The boy fell in and was immediately confronted by the 450-pound teenage gorilla known as Harambe, who'd been a mainstay at the zoo for over a decade.

The zoo's staff went to work immediately as a crowd looked on with both fear and curiosity, pointing their phone cameras and shouting. Two of the exhibit's three gorillas were called away successfully, but Harambe remained focused on the scared little boy. Eventually, the gorilla began dragging the child around the enclosure, even pushing him down at one point. Every time the child tried to crawl away, Harambe would pull him back and pin him down. It eventually became obvious that the animal was not going to let the child go peacefully, and the zoo made the only decision that made sense at the time.

With one fatal shot, Harambe was killed by the zoo's staff, in one of the most difficult decisions the institute had ever had to make. When it was over, Harambe was dead and the child was safe.

But that was just the beginning.

The national outrage was swift and severe. Petitions were filed. Memes were generated. The topic dominated the airwaves and talk shows for weeks. People around the country were questioning why the zoo had to kill the gorilla in order to save the child. Many people asked why tranquilizers weren't used, and many others insisted that the child was in no danger and that Harambe was simply protecting the boy from the loud and rambunctious crowd. Many others pointed fingers at the mother, who apparently is the only mother on the planet to have ever lost sight of her speedy child for a whole five seconds (if the internet is to be believed).

Blind outrage ruled the world wide web. No one cared about facts. Every single claim the zoo made in defense of its decision was completely ignored. Tranquilizers were not used because they don't work like they do in movies; they take several minutes to take effect and that's usually preceded by extreme agitation, which the animal almost surely would have taken out on the child. Every zookeeper and biologist in the world also agreed that whether the child was being "protected" by the gorilla was extraordinarily subjective, with many pointing out that the animal had suddenly taken ownership of the boy and that it could have easily led to a Lenny and a rabbit situation, wherein the child was accidentally killed. This was, after all, an animal that could crush a coconut by balling its fist. It would've taken very little effort to accidentally snap the boy's neck or tear off his arm. Others pointed to the crowd and how the zoo made no effort to disperse it, and how the gorilla would have calmed down if they simply had. No one seemed to care about the fact that getting a crowd of people all hoping to have the next hot viral video to peacefully leave an area is an impossible task.

For a few weeks in the Spring of 2016, everyone was suddenly a backseat primatologist. Keyboard warriors made tributes to Harambe and sent death threats to the child's mother. All of this despite even the caretaker who raised the gorilla from birth saying that there was no other viable option. Everyone suddenly felt that they, from behind their computer screen, knew more about primate behavior than the Cincinnati Zoo and every actual real scientist in the world. Even the legendary Jack Hanna weighed in, saying that he "one thousand percent" agreed with the zoo's decision. Naturally, the internet called Jack Hanna, who had been loved and respected before that, an idiot and a traitor.

The Cincinnati Zoo had to make a split second decision. They had to decide if they were going to hold a press conference to announce the death of a gorilla or a press conference to announce the death of a child. They chose the former, but America had chosen the latter. As a stepparent, I found the situation sickening, but I'll keep my personal feelings aside and be really passive aggressive about it instead.

People used the incident, like the SeaWorld accident with Dawn Brancheau, to push their ideologies. Suddenly people wanted zoos gone, and some even argued, disgustingly, that it was better to let the gorilla kill the boy since humans outnumber gorillas so vastly. (I wish I was kidding about that last sentence, but sadly I am not). Some civil rights groups were claiming that shooting the gorilla was an example of white privilege (because they thought the child was white at first), then reversed their course when they found out the child was black and claimed that the national outrage over saving the child was an example of white privilege. Practically everyone used the incident either as ammunition for their political agendas or as a stepping stone toward a figurative moral pedestal.

What can laughably be called "discussions" ran rampant on the internet, with every side of the argument calling the other side an idiot…all of this despite *no one* having any actual knowledge of the situation at hand. *The Daily Mail,* a British-based tabloid, even ran a story about the alleged criminal background of the boy's father, who had been arrested for a minor drug conviction *ten years earlier*, apparently using a small flaw in someone's character as justification for their child's safety not being as important as an animal's life.

Imagine, for a moment, if the zoo had done what so many said should have been done: that they had done nothing, or only worked to get Harambe away from the child and not "just shot the thing," as so many people said they had done in an attempt to belittle the arduous decision the zoo had to make. Imagine if the child had been seriously hurt or even killed. Imagine the outrage that would have resulted from *that*. People would have rioted in the streets of Cincinnati, internet mobs would compare it to Hurricane Katrina wherein the institution cared more about saving an animal than people—it would have been a complete disaster and even more ammunition for activist groups.

At the end of the day, the Cincinnati Zoo did the only thing it could do. It wasn't an easy decision. It was a modern day Kobayashi Maru, a no-win scenario where a group of trained professionals (unlike the internet mob that condemned them) took the only logical course of action.

The two events—the Harambe and SeaWorld accidents— are illustrative of both the human tendency to be extraordinarily hypocritical if it means being able to fabricate outrage, and that even the most well-trained animals are still animals, and are extremely dangerous. Thus, Anna Harding's terror when getting in the water with Brody cannot be understated. The two prior incidents involved animals depicted as cute and cuddly and smart. Great White sharks, on the other hand, had been given nicknames like "the white death" and "demon fish."

Obviously, Anna Harding did not want to end up like others before her; an anecdotal statistic to be mentioned by authors in future books.

"Once the shark calmed down, did you notice anything wrong with it?" I asked. "Like any health problems?"

"Initial observations were fairly positive," Anna Harding

said. "No discoloration or any obvious scars."

"Scars from fights with other sharks?"

"No, that isn't something that really happens naturally. Just because they're solitary animals doesn't mean they're aggressive toward their own species. The scars on Great White sharks are typically around the mouth where they've been hooked, or even bullet wounds. It sadly isn't uncommon that a group of drunk fishermen out on a boat might take a few potshots at a passing shark."

"So it looked healthy?"

"Not quite. There wasn't a lot of physical damage. We didn't see any finrot or anything. But there was a serious Pandarus problem." Dr. Harding explained that Pandarus actually referred to *Pandarus spp copepoda pandaridae.* Copepods are the small crustaceans that many people keep in home aquarium live rock as a food source. However, they can also serve as a parasite to larger fish. "It wasn't a horrible case, but it was there. Imagine strands of spaghetti hanging out from beneath the shark's gills. That's what it looked like."

"How'd you get rid of it?"

In a home aquarium, parasites are dealt with by using a mixture of specialized chemicals. Many of these chemicals contain copper, which is lethal to invertebrates, thus killing the attached copepods, so any infected fish traditionally have to be kept in quarantine housing. However, adding gallons of copper into Brody's tank wasn't an option.

"Well, we couldn't exactly scrape it off," Dr. Harding said. "So we introduced a more natural form of pest control."

Remoras are a type of flat, streamlined fish that usually

grow about five inches long and are distinguished by their sucker-like mouthparts. These are also sometimes called "sharksuckers" for reasons that will become obvious. These animals lack a swim bladder, which allows other fish to float at a specific depth without having to expend energy to swim, and thus use their mouths to latch onto a host for transport. These hosts include rays, whales, and sharks.

The remora and its host will live in symbiosis. The tiny fish, once latched on, then eats the parasites that might otherwise cause the host harm. (It has also been categorically proven that a majority of the remora's diet consists of the feces of its host. So, there's that...). Some remoras even make their residence in their host's mouth or under their gills. Regardless, they serve as the perfect biological cleanup crew and ideal parasite-removers.

"So you introduced a batch of remoras to help combat the parasites. Can't get any more natural than that," I observed. "The shark didn't just eat the remoras? Those have got to be some brave little fish...I see a giant monster, my first instinct isn't to go up and kiss it."

Harding faked a laugh for my benefit (I'm certain). "It does happen, but it's very rare. Remoras are really too small to make meals out of, and sharks don't chew. They tear off chunks of flesh and swallow whole, like crocodiles. So eating a remora would be pretty tough, since they wouldn't be able to suck it down. I've actually only seen it happen one time, in some viral video, and it was a small bullshark."

The remoras worked quickly once they were introduced to Brody's pool. Within a few days, the shark was free of most external parasites.

"Now the problem was feeding," Dr. Harding said.

"That's always the biggest challenge when trying to keep Great Whites, or any large pelagic sharks, really. They don't want to eat. We think of them as these monstrous eating machines, but they can get stressed out in a new environment quite easily and refuse any food."

"But he did eat eventually."

"Eventually, yes. Salmon steaks. Big ones. It was a sort of 'hallelujah' moment. It took almost two weeks. It was at the point where I was sleeping in the office almost every night, and I had actually started working on my report recommending SeaLand release the shark back into the wild. Then, one day, he just came up and grabbed a chunk of salmon."

"I imagined you were relieved."

"A part of me was. I was glad he was eating and had a clean bill of health and had stopped hitting his nose on the side of the pool, for the most part. But there was another part of me that almost hoped he wouldn't eat so I could justify releasing him to James. Oh well. History's history."

Approximately 31 days after Brody the giant Great White was taken from Murrell's Inlet, he finally appeared to be adjusted to his new home. He was eating regular meals, the water was stable, and contractors were already quoting James Warren for modifications to the amphitheater around Brody's exhibit.

The next step was to figure out how to put SeaLand's new monster fish on display.

8
Fishing for Profits

July 29, 2015 was the day that Brody's exhibit, the Domain of the King, was scheduled to open at SeaLand of Myrtle Beach. The marketing department had been working on overdrive for a month, creating brochures and graphics for promotional items. It was a ridiculously arduous process, with a team of several "marketers" — typically millennials who were "experts" at posting Facebook statuses—constantly bickering over the smallest minutiae. Someone wants to change the placement of a comma in one paragraph and it becomes a much bigger to-do than anything should ever become. Someone prefers the shade of blue in the sky to be a tone or two lighter than what's currently there and suddenly that goes through all the necessary channels instead of just doing it.

"Marketing is such a headache because there is no one right answer," Warren told me near the middle of our interview at the Giant Crab seafood restaurant. "It's so subjective. One person has one idea, the other person has another. I prefer numbers and objectivity. I don't like debate as it is, so to listen to people arguing over tiny little things that really don't matter in the long run is torture." Warren described an afternoon in which he watched emails from two of SeaLand's marketing leads go back and forth, as he had visibility over all emails. "They were seriously going back and forth about the placement of the words 'Domain of the King' on the pamphlet…should they go near the top, or a few inches from the top. One guy argued that if it's at the top, people's eyes might not 'drift far enough upward,' while the other guy argued that if it was closer to the middle, then it might obscure the shark and leave a bunch of empty space at the top. My answer to all of it was 'Who really gives a damn?' It was ridiculous. And these are people who are being paid very well…to discuss word placement on a freaking flyer that will end up in the trash anyway."

Warren didn't like the marketing department. He saw them as kids who actually thought using social media was going to bring in business. He was old school in that regard, for certain; he'd rather rely on word of mouth and press coverage. He'd been taking calls from various local networks since they'd made their press release announcing SeaLand's intention to display Brody. As expected, many calls were from various animal rights groups, and every time he picked up the phone he'd reply with a scripted paragraph whipped up by the PR department.

He tried to stay out of the marketing side. At one point, he'd just started blindly signing approval forms or not even opening the proofs he'd receive via email for various products. There were Brody plushies, mugs, water bottles and a selection of t-shirts, all featuring pictures of Great Whites that he knew weren't actually Brody, but the kids would like them all the same. The markups were ridiculous, he knew, but that was just part of the business. Charging $30 for a shirt that cost SeaLand maybe $5 may have sounded unethical, but it was the price necessary to keep the park in business and its employees paid. For the most part, he was satisfied with what the department was doing, even if he thought on more than one occasion that they spent too much time worrying about matters he deemed trivial.

But there was one thing that he agreed with them on wholeheartedly.

"The tank was boring," Warren said. "Plain white walls, plain bottom, just a perfect circle. It looked like a pool your neighbor might have in his backyard, albeit it a lot bigger. We had to do something about that. Brody wasn't enough. As fantastic as it was having a Great White shark on display, the reality was that he spent most of the time just swimming in a big circle around a big empty space. People would get bored. Fast."

"You didn't think that having one of the most iconic animals in the world on exhibit would be enough?" I asked.

"No. Not in today's world. Thirty years ago, sure. But today's generation is a lot harder to please. Six-year-olds carry devices in their pocket allowing them to access virtually any piece of information in the world within seconds. A big, empty, boring pool was simply not going to cut it. We needed to commercialize. Our park depended on it. Jobs depended on it. *Nature* depended on it."

It was impossible not to perceive some superiority complex in Warren's words as he told me about how much different conservation programs cost to fund and what Brody's exhibit could do for them. You'd get the idea that, if not for Warren's single-handed efforts, then many of the ocean's great creatures would cease to exist.

In a way, he was right. Though it's a reality than many,

particularly on the fat left side of the political spectrum, refuse to accept, zoos and aquariums have been an absolute godsend for wildlife. That fact may seem counterintuitive on the surface, as these institutions are often criticized for taking animals from their homes and putting them in cages. However, a vast, vast, *vast* majority of animals in zoos are born in captivity thanks a number of breeding programs and only very few are actually taken from the wild.

Imagine, for a moment, the following animal species: Mountain gorilla, south China tiger, Sumatran elephant, orangutan, western lowland gorilla, bonobo, chimpanzee, giant panda, loggerhead turtle, Yangtze porpoise, African wild dog, black-footed ferret, Indian elephant, snow leopard, dugong, giant tortoise, marine iguana, Lorde Howe stick insect, black softshell turtle, Hawaiian crow, axolotl, oryx, fringe-limbed tree frog, Chinese alligator, paddlefish, sturgeon, golden mole, all species of echidna, 26 species of lemur, Philippine crocodile, radiated tortoise.

These are some of the 4,574 species the International Union for Conservation of Nature and Natural Resources recognizes as critically endangered and would probably be extinct if not for the conservation efforts funded by zoos and aquariums.

While it's easy to criticize zoos who fail to keep their animals healthy and safe—and there are many, as undoubtedly all apples contain a few bad seeds—behind the comfort of a keyboard, it is impossible to understate the importance of their role in raising awareness for endangered creatures and fighting for their protection.

Say what you want regarding zoos based on reading half of a biased headline and false stereotypes, but there is one fact that is inescapable even for the most bitter internet mob: if not for the wildlife programs paid for by the cost of your admission, many of your favorite animals would not exist. If zoos suddenly disappeared, so would most of the species you see in them.

"That's the point we really needed to hammer home," said James Warren. "Yes, we took this animal out of its environment, but look at the bright side. We're keeping it safe, we're keeping it healthy, and all the money it brings in is going to save thousands of wild ones and maybe even keep this species from extinction. That's the end game here. I drive a Camry, okay? Not a Mercedes or a Porsche. Yes, putting Brody on display is about making money. But the point that people like to miss, or I should say, the one they like to *ignore*, is where that money goes."

"So, you needed to make Brody's tank more attractive. More natural looking," I said.

"Yes. Originally I wanted an artificial reef to give the exhibit some color, but Ana shot that down really fast."

Artificial reefs had been used by both home aquarists and public aquariums for decades. The National Aquarium in Baltimore recently used one while upgrading their Blacktip Reef exhibit. It is just what it sounds like: weighted plastic sculpted into the shape of various corals and colored with an acrylic latex paint to give them a vibrant, natural appearance. As technology improved over the years, so has the appearance of these reefs, and they serve as a much more cost-effective alternative to using actual coral. Some reefs even incorporate anemones made of silicone rubber that move around in the current, or a variety of copepods to call the reef home and make it appear more "alive."

"What was the problem with using an artificial reef?"

"Three things. First was installation. Almost all reefs have to be installed while the tank is empty and dry. We'd have to use divers to install the reef and that isn't a great idea with Brody, obviously. The second thing was that the shark could hurt itself on one of the sharp edges of the fake coral. It's a big, tough animal, but Ana could already see it getting too close to the tip of some coral and slicing open its belly. The third issue was water displacement. A good looking reef takes up a lot of space. We were already pushing the size limits of the pool as it was, so adding a big reef display would've just taken up more room that we couldn't really afford. So, after having what I might call a 'colorful' discussion with Dr. Harding, we scrapped the reef idea. But it worked out, though."

"It worked out?"

"Yes, because Great Whites are open ocean animals anyway. They don't spend a whole lot of time near reefs, which tend to form closer to the shore. Our solution to the aesthetic problem also led to creating an enclosure that more closely matched Brody's actual environment."

"And that solution was…"

"Marine sand."

Marine sand had been used as a substrate by all forms of aquaria for, well, decades (much like artificial reefs). Unlike the sand found on the beach, "artificial" marine sand is often composed of aragonite—a mineral commonly found in seashells. As well as giving an aquarium the appearance of an "open ocean," with a natural-looking seafloor, marine sand serves numerous other purposes. It often discourages the growth of algae, keeps the pH levels up, and serves as a medium for beneficial bacteria which help remove harmful particles from the water and aid in filtration.

"You can't just dump marine sand into the exhibit, though," Warren said. "We had to order it in bunches and mix it in buckets with seawater first, so it was damp and heavy. If we just dumped in dry sand, it would've clouded the water and probably tore Brody's gills apart before it finally settled on the bottom."

For days, the staff at SeaLand would mix buckets of marine sand with saltwater until the mix resembled thick, wet concrete. Then, one team would lure Brody to an area of the tank away from another team, who was dumping the sand into the water. It took only a few seconds to sink, and any floating sand was pressed down with paddles. More than once, Brody would come to investigate, but it was otherwise a relatively easy process. Once the entire bottom had been filled with about six inches of sand, the enclosure looked very much like the open sea.

"We used pure white sand so Brody's black body contrasted really well," Warren said. "When we were finished, we tossed in some random rocks, maybe the size of footballs, here and there just to make it look a little more natural. It was simple aquascaping, but effective, and the shark didn't seem to mind."

"Aquascaping" is a relatively new term floating around and refers to the hobby of designing aquariums to look as beautiful as possible. Some aquascapers preferred naturalistic aesthetics, as most public aquariums do, while others may go for a more surreal appearance.

The internet has been a boon for the hobby, with many sites holding contests with varying categories. It is arguable that it has become a legitimate type of artwork, a craft so popular that the Aquatic Gardeners Association currently has over a 1,000 members.

One of aquascaping's pioneers is a man by the name of Takashi Amano. In the '90s, Amano introduced the world to the "nature" style of aquascaping, which is inspired by Japanese gardening and employs attempts to mimic naturalistic landscapes. One famous example is the mountain range aquarium, which uses miniature "mountains" made of sharp stone, covered in aquatic moss to simulate trees.

In modernity, aquascaping has only become more complex, with hobbyists introducing all sorts of different styles. Reef aquariums have become immensely popular, if expensive and difficult, with many keepers going for as much color as possible. A lesser-known but equally stunning subset of the practice uses paludariums, which combine water and land in a single tank. Paludariums may include a miniature reconstruction of a jungle riverbank, with Amazonian fish swimming below the waterline and a variety of lizards or frogs living in the plants above it.

Luckily, James Warren understood the limitations of Brody's tank, and was satisfied with their simulation of an open sea.

"We added a bunch of smaller fish to the tank to go along with the remoras. All too small for Brody to eat, of course," Warren said. "All in the name of making the pool look a little more natural and less, like, well less like a pool."

"James lives in a world of spreadsheets and budgets and profits," Anna Harding would tell me later on. "He didn't see the stress that all the modifications to the enclosure put on Brody. Either that or he chose not to acknowledge it for the sake of some greater good. Any idea how hard it was to keep that shark away from one side of the tank while the contractors dumped sand into it? We had to practically scare him. His stress levels had to be through the roof, which can be deadly for many fish. Their systems shut down. They become more vulnerable to disease. Stress is a death knell, and James seemed to have no problem dishing it out for the sake of some extra dollars on the bottom line. I tried to compromise with a lot of things, but I was adamant against making any modifications to the pool. I lost that battle."

During the interview with Warren, I would ask him why he felt it was so important to squeeze as much money out of Brody's attraction as possible. While the conservation angle was brought up—and SeaLand undoubtedly contributed heavily to that enterprise—there was another issue that had previously escaped my mind.

"SeaLand of Myrtle Beach currently employs four hundred and nine [409] people," Warren explained. "We had been bleeding money for years. Every person I have to lay off is a person whose life I've potentially ruined. It isn't just the programs, it isn't just the conservation, it's the economy. People depend on us for a livelihood. And I was in charge of making sure they got to keep that livelihood.

"You want to look at me and see a monster because I wanted to market our shark? Fine, go ahead. But you get to look the people in the eye you have to fire and tell me you wouldn't do the same damn thing. There are people employed here who have dreamed about working with animals and sea life their entire lives. People who have dreamed about contributing to conservation and research and educating the public. This is the only opportunity some of them will ever have and I'm going to do everything in my power not to take that from them, activists and their fabricated outrage be damned. You know how much money we pump into this economy here in Myrtle Beach? People want to complain about there not being enough jobs, yet those same people also want to destroy them based on some delusional sense of self-righteousness."

Every major zoological institution typically produces an annual impact report. This report, which is made public, details how much money was generated by the zoo or aquarium and how that money was spent. Reading one of these reports paints a very, *very* different picture than the one that many anti-zoo internet mobs would like you to believe about some of your favorite attractions. While SeaLand's obviously pales in comparison due to its relative obscurity, the National Aquarium in Baltimore's 2015 impact report is impressive enough to make even the harshest critic at least *think* about reconsidering their stance.

In 2015, programs sponsored by funds from the National Aquarium were able to remove 130,000 pieces of marine debris from our oceans, such as plastic bottles or other trash; initiated protections for nearly 5,000 *miles* of coastline; and generated nearly *$314 million* for the local economy, not to mention the hundreds of jobs and thousands of volunteer opportunities it created.

"There is a much bigger picture here that a lot of people don't want to see, because it doesn't fit their own personal narrative of what a zoo is," Warren said. "That's why we wanted to get as much money as we could out of this shark. I never said it was easy to do some of the things we did, from an ethical standpoint, but I'll always pull the lever on the trolley if I have to. Without hesitation."

James Warren had referenced the infamous "trolley problem," a classic thought experiment introduced in the 1960s. In the trolley problem, a runaway train is heading straight for a group of five people tied to the tracks ahead. They'll surely be crushed by the speeding locomotive if nothing is done. Luckily, you're near a switch that can divert the train to another track. *However*, the catch is that there is one person tied to that other track.

Your options are thus: You can do nothing and let the five people die while the one person lives, or you can pull the lever and save the five people, yet the one person's death is *your fault*.

From a simple utilitarian standpoint, the answer is obvious: flip the switch and trade one life for five. But it's much more complex than that when we begin to examine the *moral accountability* of the person given the option to flip the switch. The person *can* do nothing and, provided they did not feel responsible for the five people who meet their untimely demises, they are off the moral hook. Meanwhile, by flipping the switch, they have saved five people, but *have directly caused the death* of another person.

It is our empathy, emotion, and sense of moral obligation that make the trolley problem so difficult...at least for most people. Do we turn a blind eye and let nature take its course, yet have no blood on our hands? Or do we intervene and have to live with the guilt of being directly responsible for someone's death?

James Warren believed in intervening.

"We thought about incorporating a red light so we could

even do a night exhibit night shows after dark, and bring in even more income from Brody," Warren said. Red lights are commonly used by keepers to simulate night time during the day time to coax out nocturnal animals such as bats. Red light is very difficult for many animals to see, and as such fools them into believing it is dark while still being bright enough for people to observe them.

"Would Brody fall asleep?" I asked. "Wait, *do* sharks sleep?" What seems like an odd question is complicated by the fact that sharks must keep water moving their gills at a constant rate, so on those terms, it would seem that sleep would be lethal.

Some sharks had developed a solution to this mobility problem by having spiracles behind their eyes (of all places) to help pump water through their gills even when they are at rest. This can still be seen in many bottom-dwelling sharks such as nurse sharks. However, the Great White's spiracles had become vestigial over the years and thus solely rely on ram ventilation—having to constantly move around in order to keep water flowing through them.

The sleep patterns of pelagic sharks, despite decades of research in both the wild and captivity, are still a complete mystery, even here in 2016. There are reports of Great Whites resting in front of currents so that water passes through their gills, but these are unsubstantiated. Some researchers believe that sharks do not ever enter deep sleep, but rather a sort of "rest mode," where they swim on autopilot while most of their brain rests. Others believe that many partake in what is dubbed "yo-yo swimming." Yo-yo swimming is when a shark swims to the surface, then lets itself go limp and rests as it descends.

"Nobody really knows," Warren explained. "One of life's little mysteries. Who knows, maybe Brody can help us answer that question."

The stage was set. The contractors were finished making adjustments to Brody's pool and were hard at work at creating the surrounding exhibits. The idea was to make the entire section with the pool dedicated to Great White sharks, the Domain of the King, indeed.

It was almost time to open the king of the seas to the public. Two and a half months after Tropical Storm Ana delivered its prize, SeaLand of Myrtle Beach was ready to put one of the greatest predators the world has ever known on display.

It's a decision they'd ultimately regret.

9
Beasts of the Deep

D r. Anna Harding led me through what can best be described as the "ruins" of the Domain of the King; an area of shops and exhibits surrounding Brody's pool. The place was littered with construction equipment such as ladders and hammers and saws, clear plastic tarps swinging in the breeze as they hung from partially deconstructed kiosks and shops.

"We're tearing this whole area apart," Anna Harding said as she led me into a small exhibit hall, pictures of Great Whites on either side, adorned with fun facts. "Eventually we're going to turn it into a sea lion exhibit." Brody's currently-empty tank was, during my visit, filled with contractors creating faux rock formations. The plan is to have a sea lion exhibit open by next year. It may even be open by the time this piece goes to print.

The entrance to the exhibit hall was framed by a massive set of shark jaws. Anna and I walked under them, and it truly felt like we were entering the belly of a great beast. The tunnel was full of little displays, including little model sharks, and one side was made of glass, offering an underwater view of what was once Brody's pool.

"The first day we opened, this was the most popular spot

in the park," Anna said as we looked out through the large observation window. At the moment, our view consisted of the contractors joking around with each other while standing in a dry pool. The bottom was being filled with brown gravel, whereas sand had been laid when Brody occupied the pool.

"I imagine it was," I replied. "I'd much rather see the shark from down here then from up there."

"You could barely move in here. And when Brody swam slowly past the window? That, I tell you, was a hell of a moment. It was much more incredible in person than the YouTube videos let on. In that first week, we had more visitors than we'd had in six months."

The opening of the Domain of the King made national news. I remember watching the story on the local Fox network in Washington, DC. I remember seeing video clips of the very hall in which I now stood, filled with euphoric kids and popping flashbulbs.

I also remember the protestors. Claiming that SeaLand was an evil organization, that it didn't care about marine life, that James Warren was the zoological equivalent of Bernie Madoff, and so on and so forth. There weren't many at first, but they'd slowly grow in number...

"Unfortunately, it didn't last," Anna said morosely. "By the end of August, we were already seeing major attendance dips, and not just because of the normal mid-season decline." Because of Myrtle Beach's tropical climate, SeaLand was able to stay open longer than most parks farther north. Even September could see temperatures reach the high 90s, and it didn't really start getting cooler until mid-November.

"People lost interest that quickly?" I asked. It was becoming increasingly obvious that the public had been spoiled in recent decades by technological advances beyond the imagination of even the most optimistic science fiction of the 19th and early 20th centuries. As a result, we got bored much more easily than we had in time past. The synopsis of the 2015 film *Jurassic World* revolved around this fact, as the director initially pitched the film as such: Imagine a *Tyrannosaurus rex*, the greatest predator to have ever walked the earth, is tearing into a goat…yet teenagers have their backs turned to it as they text away or check their Facebooks. While the film itself wasn't my favorite, and I'm sure you're tired of me making *Jurassic Park* references, the idea of the general public losing interest, very quickly, in even something as astounding as a Great White shark was not completely farfetched.

"You could say that, though I think a lot of that had to do with their expectations not being met," Anna explained. "The Great White is iconic. It's always depicted as a monster. In movies, TV shows, books…it's always the big bad, the main villain. But the real thing is sort of, well, boring to most people who don't have an actual vested interest in sharks. Obviously, anyone who loves them could watch Brody for hours, but people who just want to be entertained found it hard to watch a big fish swim in circles for very long. And then there was Meg, which we closed down as soon as we realized was a problem."

"Um, Meg?"

Anna led me around the corner of the hall, which opened up into a much larger room. Inside was a model skeleton of the largest shark I'd ever seen. It was 60 feet long with jaws that could swallow a sedan whole and rows upon rows of teeth larger than my hand. The leviathan hung from the ceiling and casted a menacing shadow over my guide and I. This was a shark that could eat Brody. This was a shark that could sink a warship.

This was the largest, most ferocious predator that had ever lived: *Carcharodon megalodon*, or simply the Megalodon.

Reaching estimated lengths of over 60 feet, the Megalodon roamed the primordial seas and feasted on *whales* during the Cenozoic era, approximately 25 million to 3 million years ago—relatively recent in the grand scheme of geological history. Looking almost identical to a Great White shark, only much longer and more robust, Megalodon's cosmopolitan distribution across the globe made it the undisputed ruler of the ocean and the stuff that nightmares are made of. The tales of monsters from the depths of the great abyss by ancient sailors pale in comparison to what the Megalodon—a creature that not only existed but was very common—was capable of.

The very first depiction of a Megalodon came in 1667 from Nicolas Steno, a Danish naturalist who is considered one of the founders of modern geology and one of the first to challenge the prior assumptions that fossils "grew" in the ground, a relic of the theological era of human history and similar to biogenesis. Megalodon teeth had been pulled from cliff faces for years prior, but were assumed to be the fossilized remnants of ancient tongues or the scales of large snakes. It wasn't until Steno published his book *The Head of a Shark Dissected* that the realization set upon the scientific world: these were very, *very* big teeth belonging to an animal of unimaginable size.

It wasn't until 1835 that Megalodon was actually classified, presumably because it was considered too nightmarish to actually exist. (That is my own observation and not an official account). Swiss biologist Louis Agassiz named the creature in his cleverly-titled work *Research on Fossil Fish*, and put Megalodon into the *Carcharodon* genus because of its uncanny resemblance to modern Great Whites.

Because Megalodon was a cartilaginous fish, like modern sharks, very little fossils remained behind, and scientists are as such forced to use their teeth to estimate the complete size of the animal. Great White sharks are often used as a basis for modern reconstructions of Megalodon because of their resemblance.

1909 saw the very first attempt to estimate the size of the Megalodon, and the results were a little off from what we know today. Bashford Dean, an American zoologist, put the creature at around 98 feet—absolutely enormous and matched only by the blue whale, *Balaenoptera musculus*, which is currently the largest animal on earth. In 1973, ichthyologist John Randall used the enamel height of Megalodon's tooth to estimate a length of a relatively tame 43 feet (though still more than double the size of some of the largest modern Great Whites). However, it was later determined that the enamel height did not necessarily directly correspond with the length of the animal, and more advanced measurements were taken in 1996 that yielded an estimated length of 52 feet.

In 2002, Kenshu Shimada developed arguably the most sophisticated technique for estimating Megalodon's length. It took into consideration crown height, enamel height, the slope of the tooth, and numerous other variables that are too boring to list here (and also too complex for me to understand). Using Shimada's method, researchers in 2010 came to a consensus on the exact average length of a Megalodon: 59 feet, with the largest *known* specimens reaching about 66 feet.

The Megalodon was the natural predator of even large whales. Despite depictions in science fiction, the shark did not coexist with dinosaurs, so the digital artwork all over the internet depicting the animal breaching the surface and dragging an oblivious tyrannosaurus to its watery grave are pure (if awesome) fantasy. In 2008, the same researchers who determined the initial bite force of the Great White shark extrapolated their results and estimated that the Megalodon bit with conservative estimate of around 108,000 newtons (remember that the Great White bites with 18,000 newtons). More gracious estimates put the number closer to 182,000 newtons. The fact that the animal is believed to have attacked by grabbing on and then shaking its head back and forth only increases the total force the beast employed while hunting its prey.

Even small Megalodon teeth can easily be larger than your palm. Megalodon teeth are a prized collector's item. I actually have several myself, collected (illegally) from Calvert Cliffs State Park, near where I grew up in Southern Maryland. The local museum, the Calvert Marine Museum, even has a fabricated skeleton of the Megalodon, which has provided a great photo op for me and my family over the years. I remember being fascinated by the skeletal remains of the mighty animal, like the ghostly remnants of a great leviathan, far more dangerous than even the sea monsters from the fairytales of ancient seafarer's could claim.

Most scientists agree that Megalodon was the most formidable predator ever to live on the planet. The scars from its teeth can be found in the bones of large whales. There was literally no animal on earth it could not call prey. An elephant too close to the shore would've been nothing short of a snack. It was the closest thing to Cthulu—the otherworldly sea monster from Lovecraft's tales of horror— the world has ever seen.

"Can you imagine putting this thing in a tank?" I said, only half-joking.

"Trust me," Anna Harding said as we looked up at the behemoth, "if it were alive today, there'd be some billionaire, somewhere in the world, hiring people to catch it."

Thankfully, most people believe that the last Megalodon went extinct several million years ago, probably thanks to a combination of a decline in its food supply and global cooling trends. However, there are a group of fringe scientists and couch truthers who are adamant about the idea that, however unlikely, a population of Megalodon sharks still roam today's oceans. And most of this speculation originated with a very curious discovery in the 19th century.

In 1872, the crew of the HMS *Challenger* collected a Megalodon tooth that seemed to only be partially fossilized. The *Challenger*, of course, was the 200-foot-long flagship of the famous Challenger Expedition, which was one of the greatest scientific endeavors of all time. The expedition covered nearly 70,000 nautical miles of ocean and led to a number of firsts for science, including the sounding of Challenger Deep, the deepest point in the world.

The Megalodon tooth discovered by the challenger sat in relative obscurity, nothing more than a museum's curiosity, until 1959, when researchers attempted to date it.

The results were unnerving.

Manganese dioxide dating put the tooth at no more than 10,000 years old. At that point, the estimate (like today) was that the Megalodon died off around 2 million years prior. But if an animal of that size could escape detection for so long, then the possibility existed—at least in the hearts and minds of those who regularly traversed the ocean—that a population of the creatures could still be around, hiding in the abyss.

However, it was later discovered that manganese dioxide dating was not accurate. The method essentially measured how much manganese had built up on a fossil, and used that determine the fossil's age. What researchers in the '50s failed to account for was the fact that manganese built up at varying rates, and it was very possible, indeed probable, that the curious Megalodon tooth was just as old as all the others. When radio carbon dating became the standard for dating organic matter—which measures trace amounts of remaining radiation—the tooth was resubmitted for dating, but unfortunately had too little nitrogen and was untestable. The mystery persists to this day, at least for the cryptozoologists who refuse to let it go.

Sharks can't melt steel beams, after all.

The idea that Megalodon could still exist has been explored by science fiction for decades. There have been books, movies, TV shows, and even fake documentaries on the subject. As with most truthers and conspiracy theorists, absence of proof is not proof of absence. The Discovery

Channel even took heavy criticism in both 2013 and 2014 for featuring "documentaries" concerning the possibility of Megalodon still roaming the oceans. The documentaries featured actors pretending to be scientists and bad CGI, and the network received backlash from the scientific community that, lucky for it, didn't affect its ratings.

"How exactly did this create problems for Brody's exhibit?" I asked.

"Comparison is the enemy of happiness," Anna said. It was a pretty cryptic line, and she could see in my face that I didn't understand. She dumbed it down for me. "Brody is awesome. He's a sixteen-foot Great White shark. But Meg's a sixty-foot shark. Kids see Brody, then they see this skeleton, or god forbid they see the skeleton first, and suddenly Brody isn't that impressive. Imagination will always trump reality. So we decided to close off this exhibit for a while to see if that improved the numbers. Then of course, James decided to install a little theater next to the viewing window with a documentary I certainly did not choose."

Anna led me away from Meg's skeleton and to a little booth near the viewing window into Brody's domain. Inside was a round bench and a curved movie screen.

I asked, "What did Warren show?"

"James decided we needed to make Brody seem more menacing, more dangerous. Guests were turned off when they compared him to a Megalodon, and then even more turned off when they found out we fed him salmon steaks and not live seals. They wanted blood. So James gave them blood."

Anna would go on to explain that the movie screen played a documentary concerning one of the most infamous serial shark attacks the United States had ever experienced, and had even served as the inspiration for the granddaddy of all shark franchises: *Jaws*.

The events that took place between July 1 and July 12, 1916 resemble something birthed from the mind of Stephen King. It was during this time that four people were killed, and one injured, in a series of shark attacks that gripped the nation.

On July 1, 25-year-old Charles Vansant was vacationing with his family at the resort town of Beach Haven, right along the Atlantic coastline and about 20 miles north of Atlantic City, New Jersey. Vansant had decided on a swim before dinner and took to playing with a dog that had been enjoying the surf. At around 6:25 pm, Vansant, who had been swimming in relatively shallow water, began screaming. Witnesses on the beach at the time believed that he was calling for the dog, when in reality he had been grabbed by an unidentified shark. Two bystanders bravely entered the water to free Vansant, then dragged him to shore as the shark followed the trail of blood. When they brought Vansant to safety, they'd realized with horror that one of his legs had been completely stripped of flesh, and the young man bled to death in the lobby of his hotel before medical help could arrive.

The second victim was a 27-year-old Swiss captain known as Charles Bruder. Bruder had been swimming a hundred yards from shore when he was bitten in two by a gigantic shark. Blood had clouded the water so densely that bystanders on the beach actually thought that a red canoe had capsized. He died shortly after being pulled into a rescue boat by lifeguards.

As horrific as the first two victims' deaths were, it was the third and fourth that sent the east coast into a panic. One of the victims was not only a child, but the incident occurred not along the beach or in the ocean, but in what was *thought* to be the relative safety of a creek.

Matawan Creek is several miles inland, yet even so, a shark managed to find its way in, just as Brody had found his way into Murrell's Inlet in 2015. The incident had the makings of a classic horror movie, including the initial witness that no one believed. Thomas Cottrell, a captain and local resident, reported the presence of the shark several days prior to its attacks, but this possibility was dismissed. The general consensus, at that point, had been that sharks could not make their way into inland bodies of water, so his claims were seen as pure fantasy.

However, on July 12, the townsfolk will have wished that they'd heeded Cottrell's warnings. Several local boys, including 11-year-old Lester Stilwell, were playing in the creek around 2:00 pm when they spotted something that looked like a "weathered log." Upon further examination, the boys discovered that it was actually a massive shark, and made way for the shore. While most boys escaped, Stilwell was not so lucky and was pulled under by the monster fish.

The boys who had escaped ran into town and alerted adults, who immediately assumed that Stilwell had actually suffered an epileptic seizure and could drown at any moment. Without hesitation, a man named Watson Fisher dove into the creek to recover Stilwell's body and hopefully revive him. Fisher succeeded in finding Stilwell…but the boy was already dead. While dragging the body back to the shore, the shark ambushed Fisher and tore at his arm, forcing him to let go of Stilwell's body and escape the water empty handed (no pun intended...sorry, that was dark). Unfortunately, Fisher succumbed to his injuries and died a few hours later.

The Jersey shore shark attacks were not immediately covered by the mass media. The first attack on Vansant was blamed on the shark mistaking him for the dog, which it was truly after. After the first death, James Meehan, former director of the Philadelphia Aquarium, downplayed the malevolence of the shark: "Despite the death of Charles Vansant and the report that two sharks having been caught in that vicinity recently, I do not believe there is any reason why people should hesitate to go in swimming at the beaches for fear of man-eaters. The information in regard to the sharks is indefinite and I hardly believe that Vansant was bitten by a man-eater. Vansant was in the surf playing with a dog and it may be that a small shark had drifted in at high water, and was marooned by the tide. Being unable to move quickly and without food, he had come in to bite the dog and snapped at the man in passing."

The beaches of the New Jersey shoreline reluctantly remained open. It was deemed that the death of Vansant was an unfortunate incident, but also an isolated one. The economy of the Jersey shore relied heavily on summer tourism, so like in all great science fiction horror stories, the first incident was brushed aside and business continued as usual.

It wasn't until after the second fatal attack that an epidemic was feared to be in the making. The story made front page news all over the United States. New Jersey's tourism industry had already lost over a quarter of a million dollars, which would be well over $5 million in 2015. Panic had become so widespread that a panel of experts came together on July 8, 1916 to assure the public that a third attack was all but certainly never going to happen, and that the first two attacks were a statistical anomaly. While they asked swimmers to stick close to shore, the beaches, they assured everyone, were safe.

To bring peace of mind to the swimming public and in the hopes of recouping some of their losses, local governments installed shark netting at several beaches. These nets were made of steel mesh wire and enclosed swimming areas to protect those venturing into the water. Motorboats with armed guards were employed to patrol the waters close to shore.

Even the President of the United States, Woodrow Wilson, got involved, and the House of Representatives allocated $5,000 to fund "shark hunts." Volunteers and crisis workers got together to eradicate the "shark threat" along the east coast, in what were inevitably scenes plucked straight from TV B-movies. The governor of New Jersey offered bounties on sharks to local fishermen. What resulted was the single biggest animal hunt in history. The Matawan Creek was even blown up with dynamite in an effort to kill these "New Jersey man-eaters."

Scientists initially struggled to identify the shark responsible for the second attack. In the resulting shark hunts, numerous species were caught, including blue sharks and sandbar sharks and bull sharks, which are known to enter freshwater. Of course, as we now know, the most likely culprit was indeed our old friend the Great White shark.

Michael Schleisser, a lion tamer for the circus, had an encounter with a Great White in Raritan Bay, at the mouth of the Matawan Creek, on July 14, 1916. The shark, purportedly, attempted to sink Schleisser's boat before succumbing to the beatings of a broken oar. Schleisser, who was also a taxidermist, dragged the carcass of the great beast to shore and slit it open. Inside the 8-foot shark, he found remains which were later identified to be human. There were no more shark attacks along the east coast for the remainder of the summer.

The attacks of 1916 struck a devastating blow to the reputation of sharks around the world. Before the incidents, they'd been seen as a mostly harmless curiosity, thought to be no threat to humans. The public then turned to the opposite extreme. Sharks suddenly became symbols of terror; monsters that actively hunted humans as prey. They became caricatures, stereotypical beasts that were to be avoided, feared, or even eradicated. It wasn't until more recently that the animals, thanks to the efforts of many zoos, aquariums and an influx of research, have begun to be looked at in a more positive, respectful light. Nevertheless, it is arguable that the modern image of sharks as "demon fish" can be attributed to the 1916 New Jersey shark attacks, an image that captivated the nation, and an image that James Warren of SeaLand hoped to replicate for Brody.

Soon, however, Warren would learn that he didn't need a documentary to teach kids how dangerous Brody could be.

The shark would do that himself.

10
Blood in the Water

Brody had been a disappointment in the public eye. People had paid their admission fees, endured the sweltering heat and humidity of Myrtle Beach, and stood in line for hours to see the legendary beast from the deep in person. Unfortunately, their expectations had been inflated by the portrayal of the Great White in mass media, and many were left unimpressed by a big fish swimming in slow circles.

"You could say the first accident is what really got us off the ground," Dr. Anna Harding would tell me will resignation in her voice. "The park wasn't doing as well as we'd expected. Or, at least as well as James [Warren] had expected. People wanted to see Brody jumping through hoops or eating sea lions. James would spend the night in his office looking at numbers and fighting depression. He didn't try to sugarcoat it, and I didn't rub it in. He was disappointed. The project had flamed out as quickly as it had been set in motion. We were almost ready to call the exhibit a failure, before, well...the first one."

"The first one" is a reference to the first publicized incident with Brody at SeaLand of Myrtle Beach. The accident almost led to its downfall. In retrospect, it is unfortunate that it did not.

Dr. Lindsay Firth had graduated from the University of California-Davis with her doctorate in veterinary medicine in 2014. Her specialty was not fish, but reptiles. She had been hired by SeaLand of Myrtle Beach to serve in the facility's popular Reptile House, which is home to about 100 different animals. The most popular exhibit is the Heart of the Jungle, a replica of the Amazon rainforest complete with turtles, caiman, and a green anaconda, *Eunectes murinus*. (The green anaconda, while incredibly large, is often mistaken as the world's longest snake. While it is the bulkiest, the title of longest—and arguably the meanest—actually goes to the reticulated python, *Python reticulates*.)

Dr. Firth oversaw the Reptile House and cared for its residents. She'd spent most days bandaging lizards or assisting with the various breeding programs, which while paling in comparison to larger institutions, was still fairly successful.

While attending UC-Davis, Dr. Firth's work with the rare spiny turtle, *Heosemys spinosa*, was met with acclaim. The animal, which looks like a turtle mixed with a spiky sea urchin, was successfully bred within one of Dr. Firth's programs, something that had only been accomplished a handful of times. The Amazonian turtle, like many other reptiles, is difficult to breed and has extraordinarily specific requirements and only lays up to three eggs per clutch at maximum.

Dr. Firth had quickly become one of the leading authorities on temperature-dependent sex determination (TSD), which is fairly common amongst reptiles. Simply put, TSD means that the biological sex (let's stay out of politics here and not use the word "gender") of an organism is determined by the temperature at which its egg is incubated. This phenomenon was first observed in the 1960s and is well-established in modernity, with entire books being written on the subject. The non-scientific gist is that eggs buried at extreme temperatures become males and those incubated at intermediate temperatures become females due to variance in the release of thermo-sensitive hormones during embryonic development.

In 2014, SeaLand of Myrtle Beach had hired Dr. Firth in the hopes that she could lead a breeding program for a pair of Mary River turtles, *Elusor macrurus*, it had acquired. The Mary River turtle is extraordinarily rare animal from Australia that is known for growing distinct patches of hair-like algae all over its body. This algae sometimes forms on its head, making the little turtle look like it's wearing a green wig. Though SeaLand was but a small park in comparison to others around the world, Dr. Firth saw it as a decent stepping stone in the right direction for her budding career.

Until, of course, the morning of August 28, 2015.

Lindsay Firth was not normally around Brody's pool. Sure, she had checked it out like all the other SeaLand staff members when it opened, but, as her expertise was herpetology (the study of reptiles, not the study of herpes, you sicko), she had no reason to be anywhere near the pool. As such, accounts vary as to what exactly happened that fateful morning.

The general consensus and the story Dr. Firth gave, and supported by park security footage, is that she had entered a relationship with one of the maintenance workers assigned to Brody's pool. The maintenance worker had invited Dr. Firth out onto the work island that morning so she could get an up close look at Brody, and no doubt an interesting picture for social media. Neither thought it was a big deal. Dr. Firth had handled her fair share of dangerous animals. While working as an intern in China one summer during her undergraduate studies, she had been responsible for brushing the teeth of several Chinese alligators, *Alligator sinensis*. These alligators are incredibly rare—nearly extinct in the wild—but are a staple of zoos in Asia. She had also assisted with surgery on a 105-pound Alligator snapping turtle, *Macrochelys temminckii*, one of the most aggressive and dangerous reptiles in the United States.

On the morning of August 28, 2015, Lindsay Firth was standing on the work island and was trying to take a picture of Brody on her cell phone. While I have not seen the security camera footage myself, I am told that she slipped back over the railing when the shark nudged the island. The maintenance worker she was with immediately reached in for her. She was only in the water a few seconds, but those few seconds are all it took. Brody the Great White attacked with his jaws wide.

Luck, if it can be called that, was on Dr. Firth's side that morning. (Well, at least *after* she entered the water). Somehow, the shark had not actually crunched down on her leg. Dr. Firth was able to pull it from the shark's mouth a mere millisecond before it clamped down and inevitably dragged her to her death. However, the teeth did slice most of the flesh from her leg below the knee, all the way to the ankle and parts of the top of her foot. Blood clouded the water. The maintenance worker dragged Dr. Firth, who did not scream, to the side of the pool, off the work island, and called for help.

"I didn't feel anything," Dr. Lindsay Firth would tell me over a phone interview. Her leg had been, quite literally, filleted by the shark's powerful teeth. The teeth of most sharks curve backwards into their mouths. This prevents any prey that survives the initial bite from escaping its maw. Similar adaptations can be seen going back all the way to the time of the dinosaurs. For example, the notorious aquatic *Mosasaurus*—a terrifying mix of whale and crocodile that reached 60 feet in length—actually had a set of teeth *within* its upper jaw. These teeth, called pterygoid teeth, helped keep prey in place if it needed further shredding *or* made sure that smaller prey couldn't escape the leviathan's mouth before its trip down its throat and into its stomach alive. This was a fate that was cruelly bestowed upon a young woman in the 2015 film *Jurassic World*. (No, I will *not* stop with the *Jurassic Park* references.)

Odd dietary adaptations persist amongst the oceanic realm, and while that of sharks are fairly simple (curving, serrated teeth), one of the more gruesome—and terrifying—examples of a mouth you'd never want to meet actually belongs to the otherwise-unassuming leatherback sea turtle, *Dermochelys coriacea*. The leatherback sea turtle is a colossal animal, and is in fact one of the largest reptiles in the world. While its babies are very cute and can frequently be seen throttling for the ocean after they've hatched on the beach, the adults can reach upwards of a thousand pounds and extend over nine feet in length.

For all its size and the cuteness of its hatchlings, the leatherback sea turtle's mouth hides a terrifying secret that's surely given nightmares to any naturalist who's peeked inside. Its mouth and throat are lined with thousands of spiky teeth called papillae, giving it the appearance of some miniature sarlacc. The reason for this bizarre adaptation is simple: the turtle survives primarily off jellyfish, and the papillae ensure both that the slippery meals don't get away and work to absorb any stings.

Lindsay Firth's shredded leg was treated at the nearby Grand Strand Medical Center. The maintenance worker, who was never officially named, did his best to wrap the leg in a shirt, but had no medical training. Skin grafts were used to repair the leg, but the scars remain, and Dr. Firth cannot currently walk without assistance.

"It almost felt…cold," she told me during our brief conversation. "They told me I didn't feel anything at first because of shock, but then that sort of turned into this numb, cold sensation." It is my understanding that the leg was so badly damaged that the nerves beneath the flesh were not functioning properly. As such, Lindsay Firth felt surprisingly little pain at first. But it didn't last long. "Once I was in the ambulance on the way to the hospital, that's when I really started to feel it. Once the shock wore off, and reality started setting in, it went from a coldness to a burning. I looked down at my leg and threw up."

Firth spent weeks in the hospital and spent a year on leave. At the time of this writing, she is actually planning on returning to SeaLand, but will not be hanging around any shark tanks in the near future.

James Warren was certain that the incident would lead to the closing of Brody's display. He was certain that it would scare people away and increase activist resistance to their prized exhibition.

He was only half right.

"Brody's popularity exploded," Warren told me as we knocked back beers at the Giant Crab restaurant. At this point, I wasn't sure how many I'd had. Warren explained that of course Brody's exhibit was immediately closed to the public until the legal matters could be settled, but it didn't last long.

A workers' compensation claim is typically very simple. A worker gets injured on the job, and his or her medical bills are paid as well as about two to five times more for any other punitive damages, such as missed work or scars. However, Dr. Firth's case was unique. She was not authorized to be around Brody's pool, and thus there was a chance that the compensation claim could be denied.

"I had no problem paying everything," James Warren said. "All the medical, pain and suffering, all of that. She might never walk right again. That's worth something. Even if it was her own fault."

Warren wanted to avoid the issue and have SeaLand's insurance company simply pay out, but they wouldn't budge. "We can't just take money and give it to her, it doesn't work like that. We submit the workers compensation claim to our corporate insurer, and they ultimately make the decision, usually at a hefty punch to our premium. I suggested we just pay it out. They didn't agree."

James Warren did not want a legal battle. The insurance company would claim that Lindsay Firth was not authorized or trained to be around the shark, while Firth would argue that the safety measures—notably the railing and slickness of the work island—were not sufficient. It would go back and forth and would be a PR nightmare.

"I wanted to just do the right thing and pay the girl,"

Warren said with a sigh. "Unfortunately, it was out of my hands and we couldn't afford those medical bills out of our own pocket without having to let an employee or two go. Luckily there wasn't a personal injury claim." When a zoo employee is injured, it is not uncommon for not only a workers' compensation claim to be filed but a personal injury suit against the owner of the animal that attacked, in this case SeaLand. The personal injury claims can sometimes reach as high as ten times the cost of the required medical bills, oftentimes to help with emotional damages and any lifelong therapy.

While Warren battled with the insurance company, something no one expected was coming to fruition: more and more people were coming to see Brody, and many demanding that the exhibit be reopened.

"People wanted blood, and Brody finally gave them blood," Warren said. "It was amazing what the accident did for attendance. Obviously after Firth's fall, we had to re-inspect the entire exhibit with the approval of the OSHA [which found that SeaLand had committed no safety violations]. After a few days, we reopened the pool and its popularity exploded."

Anna Harding told me, "People were much more interested in Brody now that they knew he was a killer shark. There were headlines trending all over social media about a monster shark attack at SeaLand, and no one bothered to actually read the articles and see that Lindsay [Firth] had survived and was recovering. We went from having a boring shark to a monster shark, and that's what people wanted to see. For better or worse."

Guests wanted to see the shark that had torn apart the

young woman's leg. Her injuries, while gruesome, had been exaggerated online. Brody had become an overnight sensation and the grand stands of the Domain of the King were now always full.

"Lines got so long to see Brody that we had to hire extra people to only let in a certain number at a time," Warren recalled. SeaLand also had employees walk up and down the lines peddling Brody-themed merchandise. "We suddenly had the monster on our hands that people wanted to see. But like any fad, we knew it wouldn't last long. People lose interest in things so quickly these days, so we had to work fast to make sure we could strike while the iron was hot, because it might be our only chance."

SeaLand's Great White shark—if through inflated circumstances—was finally living up to the legend that precluded it. It was now up to that little marine park to make sure they could wring every penny out of Brody and bring as much attention to their establishment as possible.

Unfortunately, it wasn't quite the attention they wanted.

11
Marketing a Monster

I knew we are on the verge of having a major problem on our hands the day Brody decided to show his teeth to the audience," Anna Harding said. We had moved into her office at SeaLand after she had finished giving me a tour of the Domain of the King's ruins.

"What do you mean by that?" I asked. "The accident with Dr. Firth?"

"No. Well. Kinda. That accident sort of created these new expectations, so more people came flooding in, but Brody still hadn't really met them. At least not until an idiot pelican decided to land right in the pool. I was on the work island when it did. I knew exactly what was about to happen. You won't believe how many people suddenly flipped out their cell phones and started filming. I just held my breath."

The video was widely available online for a while, but had recently been removed by request of a number of organizations as it could be interpreted as animal abuse. The internet is no stranger to gross-out videos. Most of them were shocking for the sake of being shocking. Then there were reaction videos to the shocking videos. And reaction videos to the reaction videos. One popular category of shocking internet videos involves animals eating other animals. Some people find it fun to toss a mouse into a tarantula cage, watch as the mouse gets brutally killed by the spider, then post the video online. There's some sort of primal joy people get out of watching death, either live or in video. When I was working at a mom-and-pop pet store in my teens, I had a coworker who found some odd sense of pleasure from dropping feeder mice into a tank with our larger fish (the species of which I cannot recall) and watching the mouse get gulped down in terror.

It is because of this bloodlust that one of the most popular videos near the tail end of summer 2015 was shot at SeaLand of Myrtle Beach, in the Domain of the King.

The American white pelican, *Pelecanus erythrorhynchos*, is a common sight around South Carolina waters. These enormous birds, which can reach five feet long and 20 pounds, fit the stereotypical image that most people probably have of pelicans. The bright white plumage is contrasted by the orange beak that can reach well over a foot long, and adorned with a fleshy pouch below. This pouch is used as a type of bucket or net for scooping up fish, which comprises the pelican's diet.

Ironically, one unlucky pelican got to experience what it felt like to be the hunted rather than the hunter. Three days after the Domain of the King had reopened and the grandstands were full of spectators, this particular pelican had decided a great place to land for a rest from its flight was Brody's pool. As the roof had not been constructed yet (and never would be), the pool was open.

"It was probably flying along the coast and over the grounds, then saw us dumping large salmon steaks on a rope into Brody's pool and thought, 'Hey, look, free food!' Idiot plopped down into the water and scooped up the salmon, but then decided not to let go even after it realized it was attached to twine."

One unique physiological adaptation of most pelicans is its ability to breathe while swallowing, as some prey may struggle on the way down its gullet. Snakes have a similar mechanism, as they can take many hours to swallow a meal. Pelicans don't chew and must swallow their prey whole. As a result, a vast majority of victims are still alive. The pelican's throat is very elastic and can expand to accept large prey (again, much like a snake). There's a gut-wrenching video available online of a pelican in London park grabbing an unsuspecting pigeon and swallowing it. The pigeon struggles all the way down, and its outline can be seen in the throat, still struggling, until it finally reaches the pelican's stomach and all goes eerily still.

"So, the stupid bird didn't understand the concept that he couldn't swallow the salmon and the twine. And he paid with his life, "Anna Harding said.

Within moments, Brody had struck from below. The water erupted, the first row of people was splashed, and all that remained after the vicious attack was a cloud of blood and feathers.

The crowd went wild.

SeaLand's staff, including Anna Harding, just looked at each other and shrugged. What could they have done?

"I had two reactions," James Warren told me. "The first was, 'Shit, now we get yet another PR nightmare to deal with.' Yeah, it was only a pelican, but activists will act like this is the only bird in history to ever get eaten by a shark and it never would have happened if we hadn't taken Brody from the ocean."

While I don't remember the exact context, James Warren once referred to the activists that constantly bombarded the internet—the keyboard warriors who wouldn't lift a finger in real life to help the causes they claimed to support—as "overreactivists." The truth that birds fell victim to sharks in the wild all the time. Seagulls, ducks, pelicans; none who landed on the water were safe from the jaws of a pelagic shark. In fact some sharks, like the infamous tiger shark, *Galeocerdo cuvier*, made seabirds a routine part of its diet. Surely, there'd be tributes and memes and whatever else the internet could dig up to the pelican, and people would use the death of such a "magnificent, graceful creature" as ammunition in their constant fight to hoist themselves upon the false pedestal of morality.

"What was the second reaction?" I asked.

"This is great. This was the first time I'd actually heard people applaud for Brody. I feel bad about the bird, sure, but this was going to really bring in a hell of an audience."

"Live feeding shows, then?"

The topic of zoos having "live feeding shows" is something less realistic than it's often portrayed as in movies and television. "Are you joking?" Anna asked, raising her eyebrows when I asked her sometime later. I wasn't, but I told her I was. She explained, "This isn't exactly the Roman empire where we can throw Christians to lions. Live feeding shows, even if Brody was just being fed fish, wouldn't go over well."

Many zoos and aquariums offer feeding shows, but usually with non-aggressive animals and never with live prey. At practically any aquarium in the country, visitors can pay to watch divers dump dead fish into a shark tank. But the key is the fact that the fish are already dead. For some odd reason, the act of killing the fish beforehand *then* feeding it to a zoo animal is fine, but the practice of just feeding the animal a live fish is frowned upon.

"We already had enough PR problems after the incident with Dr. Firth and the idiot pelican," Anna said. "A live feeding show would've had us investigated and probably fined." In truth, no one is quite sure what legal action would be taken against SeaLand, if any, if it had tried to feed Brody live prey. It's not like it is against the law. People often feed their pets at home live prey; snakes are tossed mice, large fish are given small goldfish known as "feeder fish" in enormous quantities, and spiders are given crickets. Some pet stores even sold feeder rabbits for larger pet snakes such as boas or pythons.

However, the way James Warren explained it to me right as the alcohol started to hit him during our dinner at the Giant Crab restaurant, live feeding is a lot like sex. Everyone accepts that it happens, but put it on display and it becomes something more taboo, something to be regulated.

Off topic, readers, but if you've ever heard an odder analogy, please write to me.

"Long story short, live feeding shows are off the table," Anna said. "Even though you and I both know that those would make us the most popular park in the world, for better and worse. In fact, it didn't take long for the conspiracy theorists on the internet to come out of the woodwork. The same type of people who were convinced that victims of mass shootings are actually actors hired by the government in order to push anti-gun rules are the ones who were convinced that we had planted the pelican in order to get people excited for our shark. It was ridiculous."

Nevertheless (and intentional or not), Brody's popularity went up after the accident with the pelican. Attendance had never been better, and people in the grandstands kept their cameras pointed to the sky, eagerly waiting for another unsuspecting waterfowl to take a break in Brody's pool and meet its untimely doom.

Marketing shifted from portraying Brody as an elusive, magnificent creature to portraying him as a prehistoric monster. A vertical banner was put in place next to the entrance to the exhibit, relaying shark attack statistics, with particular attention paid to Great White attacks. Since 1958, there have been nearly 3,000 unprovoked shark attacks attributing to around 550 fatalities. Numbers can be unreliable due to inconsistencies in record keeping, so I have avoided using exact numbers. Of the 550 or so (see, no exact numbers) fatal incidents, nearly 300 can be attributed to the Great White shark. This was not lost upon SeaLand's marketing team, much to the chagrin of Dr. Anna Harding.

One of the reasons that shark attack statistics are not perfect is because it is often difficult to attribute the cause of death to a shark if there is no body, or if the person died of some other way and was then bitten by a shark afterward. Many disappearances may have been because of sharks, but we'll never know.

While the Great White gets all the press, there is another shark that, because of two famous incidents involving sinking ships, may possibly be responsible for even more deaths: the oceanic whitetip shark, *Carcharhinus longimanus*, which famous naturalist Jacques Cousteau once described as the most dangerous shark in the world.

It can be generally agreed that the oceanic whitetip's reputation stems from two incidents, both during World War II. The first involved the United Kingdom's RMS *Nova Soctia*. An ocean liner carrying over 1,000 passengers, it was sunk by a German u-boat, *U-177*, off the coast of South Africa in November 1942. Over 850 of the passengers either drowned or were consumed by oceanic whiteips that had been drawn to the sinking. The second accident occurred in 1945, when the USS *Indianapolis* was struck by torpedoes from a Japanese submarine and sank in the Pacific. Of the 1,200 onboard, approximately 300 went down with the ship while most of those who survived were eaten by oceanic whitetip sharks. (In what can perhaps be interpreted as the poetic hand of fate, karma, and/or justice, depending on what side you're on, the crew of the *Indianapolis* was on its way back from delivering parts for what would ultimately be the atomic bomb dropped on Hiroshima.)

"So, the idea of shark attacks was played up by marketing," Anna Harding said. "But it was sort of this butterfly effect. Marketing a monster turned into marketing the idea of this wild, primal beast. That led to a lot more attention from animal rights groups."

"You had dealt with that before, though?"

"Right. The entire time. Since the day we had our first press release. But we still didn't have national attention. Monterey Bay Aquarium didn't have national attention. They had some little, baby sharks. We had a full-fledged Jaws. Protesting something that had brought so much attention would bring protestors attention."

It is an inescapable reality that activism is very selective. This isn't a slight to humanity, it's just how it is. More popular things get more attention and more sympathy and attract more support or ire, depending on the chosen side. It's just math. A man is gunned down in the street and it would barely make headlines, or even escape the police briefs. There are no vigils, nor any protests. But a man is gunned down in the street by a police officer—with police violence against minorities being a hot button topic of the 2000-teens—then suddenly national outrage runs rampant.

People care about exposure. What's going to help *me* the most? So while atrocities were being committed all over the United States, scores of activists descended upon SeaLand— conveniently right about the time Brody's exhibit was getting even more famous.

"But there lies the reality of too much modern activism," James Warren said. "Some people *want* bad things to happen. Because it gives them a cause. What would all those anti-smoking activists be doing if we all banded together and decided to ban cigarettes? They'd have nothing to do, and would have to find something else to take a stand against.

"We live in a time where tragedy keeps people in business. Whenever there's a school shooting, the anti-gun activists come crawling out of the woodwork, claiming they don't want violence. But deep down, let's be honest here, the violence is the only thing that gives them the exposure they so desperately want. Anti-police warriors absolutely *love* when one idiot cop out of the millions of good ones pulls his trigger a little too fast. Now they have something to point at and go 'See! I was right and you're wrong!' Liberals and conservatives lick their lips whenever there's some sort of injustice they can capitalize on. I remember being at a rally a few weeks back where a woman did everything she could to get herself kicked out. She was being rude, wouldn't let presenters speak, and even interrupted people asking questions. Then, when she was finally escorted out, she claimed prejudice and spun it into this heartbreaking story of a poor innocent woman being kicked out because of her heritage. Give me a f*cking break." Warren rolled his eyes as he spoke.

"You and I both know that she *wanted* to get kicked out. We live in a world where people intentionally provoke reactions, then try to claim victimization. My niece was a residency director at FIU, and part of her job was to mediate disputes or hear complaints. There was this girl who was really into makeup. You know, the fancy makeup. Green cheeks, blue eyes, whatever. Just her thing. No one cared. I'm a firm believer that college is all about expressing individuality, so no judgment. But, one day this same girl decided to come to class with no makeup on. Someone made an innocent comment, something along the lines of, 'No makeup today, huh?' And that turned into this girl sobbing in my niece's office because suddenly she felt she was being held to a beauty standard by the patriarchy. Ridiculous. And it waters down real problems that women face. But all those legitimate issues with social and corporate gender bias suddenly get clumped in with attention seekers."

I cleared my throat. James Warren's republican ranting was getting us a little off topic. "We're getting a little off topic," I said. Not that I didn't agree with much of what Warren was saying. I was just here to learn about sharks.

"Oh, right, sorry. Anyway, so the point I was trying to make was that activists will always make situations seem way worse than they are in order to push their own political agendas. You think they're just and righteous? Many are, but many aren't. Many are in it so they can pretend they're standing above everyone else on the moral ladder. In reality, there's nothing a lot of animal rights activists would love more than to see a woman drop her baby into a tiger cage so they can get a bunch of clicks on their angry little blog."

It sounded like Warren had an angry little blog himself. However, it would become apparent over the next few weeks that the problem with activists at SeaLand was spinning out of control. And it would soon culminate in one of the most infamous events in the history of zoos and aquariums.

12
The SeaLand Incident

T he genesis of the modern day animal rights movement can be difficult to pinpoint, but most experts (and people pretending to be experts by writing a book) can trace its inception to a group of individuals in the 1960s. These individuals, most of whom were postgraduate students at Oxford University in the United Kingdom, banded together to publish the book *Animals, Men and Morals: An Inquiry into the Maltreatment of Non-humans.* (Ironically, this book developed by Oxford students did not include an Oxford comma in its title.)

The book, released in 1971, was inspired by an essay from author Brigid Brophy from 1965. Brophy was a proponent of social reform, what many may today equate with the picketers and protestors and social media warriors who can often be seen marching through college campuses across the United States. In her essay, titled simply "The Rights of Animals," Brophy imagined a scenario where one could hang a piece of food out the window of their fourth-story apartment, wait for another person to come by and inspect the food, then hook that person, drag them up to the apartment, and gut them and eat them. While I'm certain many serial killers of the day enjoyed these fantastic scenarios in their...own way...Brophy's purpose was to put readers into the mind of an animal in an attempt to generate empathy.

The book, which shall hereafter be referred to only as "the book" because of its long title and my publisher's desire to save on ink, included many essays revolving around a number of topics that are still relevant to this day. Factory farming, using animals as medical test subjects, and even using fur were studied. The book also made mention of the moral ineptitude of both using animals as food and for labor. Patrick Corbett from the University of Sussex even went so far as to equate animal labor to the human slave labor of the American antebellum.

The word "speciesism" made its mass debut in the book (though it made a cameo earlier in a 1970 pamphlet). Speciesism is just what it sounds like: bias against members of a particular species. It was equated to racism…somehow. And, as some gender identity reformists today like to refer to sexual biology as "vague", contributor Richard Ryder referred to the idea of "different species" being a "vague" concept. (Let it be known that while the author agrees that gender identity can be vague since many consider gender a mental/societal and not a biological construct, I simply cannot allow myself to see no biological difference between members of different sexes or species).

The book was (shockingly) not received well. Ryder's argument that differences between species are mental constructs was especially panned. While it is impossible to argue against what some may interpret as spiritual connections—if you think that your soul is no different from the soul of a goldfish then more power to you—many of the articles ignored basic science in favor of radical philosophy.

Comparing species to race doesn't hold up under scientific scrutiny. A species is an entirely different organism from another species. They cannot typically interbreed without some sort of assisted mechanism. Yes, hybrids exist in nature, but these are extraordinarily rare and are exceptions, not the rule. To defy a classic *South Park* episode: no, an elephant cannot make love to a pig and produce a tiny, pig-sized elephant.

Race, however, is a different story. Different varieties of organisms can exist within one species. This is race. For example, there is only one species of domesticated dog, but there are hundreds of different varieties—pugs, bulldogs, retrievers, Chihuahuas—all look wildly different but belong to the same species. Human beings fall into the same category. We are a very genetically diverse animal, particularly when it comes to skin pigmentation, but we all belong to one species: *Homo sapien*.

The authors of the first animal rights books hoped that ethics could trump science. (*Feels before reals*, as the internet likes to say). While many dismissed the articles as agenda-fueled reformist propaganda, there were many others who would take the arguments *very* seriously, and from these convictions would sprout modern animal rights groups.

While the group at Oxford may be responsible for recent interpretations of animal activism, the philosophical question of animal rights dates back several centuries. Some of the most well-known philosophers in history touched on the subject, often with a multitude of viewpoints. The Frenchman Descartes proposed that, while humans had a sentience on par with the gods, animals were but organic machines, or "automata," without souls or true consciousness. Others, such as Nicolas Malebranche, agreed with this assumption, famously stating that animals "desire nothing, fear nothing, [and] know nothing."

The British philosopher John Locke, while not the antithesis of the non-sentient views, did at least believe that animals were capable of feeling pain. However, his reason for opposing cruelty to animals was less about compassion and more about practicality. He believed that teaching children that it was okay to harm animals would "harden them toward harming men."

In the 1800s, progress toward legislation that protected the welfare of animals, something which had been unheard of until then, was gaining steam, particularly throughout England. In 1809, a bill was introduced that protected cattle and horses from malicious wounding or mistreatment. This was a monumental step toward protecting the rights of animals, as before the bill, they were seen only as property. A person could be persecuted for harming another person's animal simply because it boiled down to property damage, but a person could not be persecuted for harming their own animal. This bill changed all of that. In the words of Lord Erskine, the punishment of cruelty to cattle and horses based only on their monetary value was a "defect in the law he wished to remedy."

In 1824, the Royal Society for the Prevention of Cruelty to Animals (RSPCA) was formed. Today, it is the largest organization dedicated to animal welfare in the world. The society is responsible for some of the first true acts of bringing illegality to animal cruelty and influenced Parliament to enact a number of laws protecting them. These include the Cruelty to Animals act in 1876 which put limits on animal experimentation and more recently the 2006 Animal Welfare Act. The RSPCA has been responsible for bringing thousands of alleged abusers before the courts since its inception and today plays one of the most active roles in the world in regards to protection of animals.

While the RSPCA has not had a record clean of controversies here and there, they have for the most part remained the gold standard for a welfare charity. They have set up a network of thousands of individuals, some paid and some volunteers, who dedicate their lives to protecting animals. They believe in the power of pets and have not pushed political agendas. They have established educational programs, rehabilitation programs, animal hospitals, all without many needless gimmicks or much sensationalism, and as a result have become one of the world's most respected organizations not just in terms of animal welfare, but in general. Their reputation, despite some of the minor dings in their moral resume (as are wont to nearly all major organizations that have been around almost two centuries), is very clean.

Then there is PETA...

Since its very early years, the organization known as the People for the Ethical Treatment of Animals have been a lightning rod for controversy. Founded in 1980, it actually saw much success during those infantile years and came to global prominence after the infamous Silver Spring Monkeys Case.

Silver Spring is a city in Maryland, just north of the District of Columbia. It's the sort of place where most people can't make a living unless you make well over six figures. Everything is high end and upscale. The mall is filled with the sort of stores you've probably never heard of if you don't have a trust fund somewhere, usually with one-word names so everyone knows how hip and trendy they are.

In the early '80s, Silver Spring was also home to the Institute of Behavioral Research. Here, Dr. Edward Taub was studying how the brain interacted with the muscles in the body. His hope was that he could find a way for people who have lost feelings in their limbs to regain control; stroke victims, people with degenerative disorders, and the like. This was groundbreaking research. Unfortunately, very little in life comes without a tremendous amount of personal sacrifice, and in this case Dr. Taub "employed" the services of 17 monkeys who would become national celebrities for all the wrong reasons.

Alex Pacheco, a member of PETA, went undercover as a technician in Taub's laboratory to examine the conditions under which the monkeys were being held.

His photographs shocked the world.

Taub had been torturing the monkeys. There isn't any way to sugarcoat it. The monkeys were having chunks of their brains cut out then having their bodies constrained on machines that wouldn't look out place in a gory R-rated snuff film. In addition, when the monkeys were not being experimented on, they were each kept in tiny cages more appropriate for hamsters, with little food and water and no sunlight or stimulation. These animals were not respected. These animals were treated like pieces of equipment and abused. There is no debate about that.

The release of the appalling photographs (which you can look up online…if you have the stomach for it), resulted in the very first police raid on an animal laboratory in the

United States. Police confiscated the monkeys and charged Dr. Taub with numerous counts of animal cruelty, many of which he was convicted. However, the convictions were all overturned when it was determined that Maryland's legislation regarding animal cruelty did not apply to federally-funded laboratories. In other words, Maryland could not legally charge itself with a crime.

Tragically, the monkeys were killed sometime later when the courts refused to grant PETA custody. However, Dr. Edward Taub's research did in fact prove valuable, and even today the techniques that were developed thanks to the experiments done on the Silver Spring monkeys have been praised for helping stroke victims regain movement.

Thanks to the incident, PETA had been transformed from a small fringe group into a national powerhouse of an organization. They remain in the spotlight to this day, but typically in much more controversial fashion. The organization frequently protests (which is an American right, albeit) and often use sensationalism to reinforce their beliefs. You'll often see followers of PETA scolding meat eaters, walking around naked, or handing out pamphlets on college campuses depicting the graphic processing of chickens that eventually become fast food nuggets (*delicious* fast food nuggets, mind you), or tossing buckets of red paint on those wearing fur.

PETA, for all their good intentions, often tend to invoke eye rolls due to their extremism. Unlike the RSPCA, PETA is frequently looked down upon by the general public for being, for lack of a better term, annoying.

However, from the seed sowed by PETA and the case of the Silver Spring monkeys grew an organization that can only rationally be described as extremist. The U.S. Department of Homeland Security even classifies the Animal Liberation Front, or ALF, as a terrorist group, and for good reason. The ALF is a guerilla organization that takes part in direct, often illegal action against those they see as being cruel to animals. Like any terrorists, their definition of "cruelty" can be stretched to fit anyone they deem an enemy.

Founded in the United Kingdom in 1976, the ALF is a leaderless organization much akin to the Underground Railroad (or at least that's how they like to be perceived). They have a habit of destroying laboratories and stealing animals from farms to be set free in the wild (where many most likely die as a result of overreliance on domestication). Unlike other organizations, ALF openly promotes violence "if necessary" against those it perceives as offenders. In the infamous words of activist Keith Mann:

"Labs raided, locks glued, products spiked, depots ransacked, windows smashed, construction halted, mink set free, fences torn down, cabs burnt out, offices in flames, car tyres es slashed, cages emptied, phone lines severed, slogans daubed, muck spread, damage done, electrics cut, site flooded, hunt dogs stolen, fur coats slashed, buildings destroyed, foxes freed, kennels attacked, businesses burgled, uproar, anger, outrage, balaclava clad thugs. It's an ALF thing!"

The organization became highly—and violently—active in the 1990s and focused much of their strategy on property damage. Numerous farms and breeding facilities were destroyed, often burned to the ground. In 1992, over 100 meat trucks were bombed using incendiary devices. In 1990, the vehicle of veterinarian Margaret Baskerville was bombed. She narrowly escaped with her life by leaping from the window of her car. A few days later, another bomb was set off near the vehicle of physiologist Patrick Headley. While Headley escaped unharmed, a toddler that was being pushed nearby suffered severe burns and shrapnel wounds.

In 2006 came one of the most egregious cases of ALF's extremism. A homemade firebomb was placed on the doorstep of a home owned by UCLA researcher Lynn Fairbanks. The bomb thankfully failed, but authorities are certain that it would have killed numerous people, the great irony being that the home was being rented out by Dr. Fairbanks to an elderly tenant. Of the attack, ALF member Jerry Vlasak essentially shrugged it off saying that there was "certainly moral justification for that." (I am not kidding. That is a direct quote. Look it up. These people are insane.)

Bombs had become a common tool of ALF. In fact, several years earlier, a journalist by the name of Graham Hall was kidnapped by several ALF members after he had gone undercover and exposed them giving him instructions on how to make bombs. Graham was tied up and beaten in the back of a truck but survived.

As a direct result of ALF's ecoterrorism, the Animal Enterprise Terrorism Act was passed in the United States. This essentially gave authorities more leeway when it came to pursuing potential domestic terrorist threats, which ALF had obviously become.

In modernity, ALF has arguably become even larger thanks to the connective power of the internet. As such, demonstrations are common. Combine the ever-present feeling of victimhood demonstrated amongst many in our current society, and the constant need for attention, what happened at SeaLand of Myrtle Beach at the end of September 2015 was not at all surprising.

"It was a simple plan," said Heather Morton, the wife of the late Sebastian Morton, as we sat down for coffee at a local Denny's. Her eyes are sunken and glassy. Her fingers shake as she holds her coffee cup. The SeaLand incident appears to still be fresh in her mind, despite happening almost nine months prior to our interview. She wears a very simple pink t-shirt and her words seem very distant and detached, as if she's speaking on the bench in court.

She is a former member of the Animal Liberation Front.

"Every plan's simple," I reply. "Until it's complicated."

On the morning of September 29, 2015, Heather Morton lost her husband to the jaws of the world's largest captive Great White shark.

"It was about two or two-thirty in the morning. I don't remember exactly," she explains, still shaking. "The plan was to clog the filter system."

"Clog the filter system?"

"Yes. The plan was to kill the shark."

Now, I know what you're thinking, reader: Why on *earth* would a group that promotes violence against those who harm animals *want to harm an animal*? The answer is simple. Brody would be a sacrifice to get people on their side. These types of fabricated attacks have unfortunately become all too common. Go online now and you can find dozens of stories of servers writing nasty notes on receipts then claiming they were written by customers. You'll find several fabricated racial attacks, including a famous incident at the University of Albany where the victims of a "racial" attack turned out to be perpetrators. You'll find even more examples of organizations damaging their own property and claiming they were victimized, all in the name of garnering sympathy for their causes.

While there is absolutely no doubt that many attacks *are genuine* (please don't pull the "Oh wow, look at this guy thinking no one ever actually is victimized!" strawman argument), it is unfortunate that they are often muddled beneath gobs of cases that are no more than glorified examples of Munchausen syndrome. (Munchausen syndrome is a condition whereby a person feigns victimhood or illness in order to draw attention to themselves.)

Everyone wants to be a hero, even if it means they have to sometimes create their own villains.

ALF was not happy with the fact that Brody was thriving at SeaLand. It went against their paradigm that animals in captivity are all suffering and unhealthy. They knew no one would take them seriously if all they did was protest. Brody had to be sacrificed. The world had to think that SeaLand had killed this beautiful creature.

Technically, because ALF is such a loose organization, there was no de facto leader and no type of obvious structure. Sebastian and Heather Morton had done most of their planning via internet forums and online chat groups. Neither had criminal records. Both had college degrees from the same university in Liberal Studies and had become embroiled in the great millennial crisis of the 21st century: drowned beneath a sea of student loan payments and a housing market that kept them renting a substandard apartment.

"We were angry at the world," Heather Morton told me. "We get angry and we start looking for people to blame. Faceless corporations, rich people, they're easy targets."

Looking for people to blame. That could have been a slogan for many of the movements many claimed as "progressive" throughout the 2000-teens. Former students had taken out massive loans to pay for college tuition under the guise of having work when they got out, only to find that the jobs simply weren't there. I—the author of this piece—was no exception to this; I spent several years after graduating college in 2011 surfing on couches and sleeping in my car until finally finding stable employment in North Carolina. I didn't own a bed until nearly two years after I received my college diploma.

However, many of my generation gave into frustration and instead of continuing to chip away at their debt or look for work in an uncertain market (I vividly remember sending dozens of job applications out per day, a hundred per week), they began looking for people to blame. Two entities came to mind: big businesses and the government. Students took to the streets to protest not being able to find work (instead of working harder to find work). Big business and Wall Street lenders were now seen as the evil empire because...they didn't give people free money? Younger people began migrating toward political candidates who promised to wipe out the debt that they voluntarily accumulated, as if the banks had physically taken their hands and forced them to sign agreements.

Many people, instead of working to solve the problems that faced them—no matter how insurmountable they seemed—decided to focus their energies instead on blaming others for them. This led to increasingly rebellious attitudes among young Americans. And this led to the SeaLand incident.

SeaLand of Myrtle Beach's capture of Brody the Great White shark represented everything that many young Americans despised. Here was a large corporation that had taken an innocent animal from its home and placed it in a cage akin to the shackles said corporations apparently put on the economy. Protests and picketers became more and more common in the days after Brody's exhibit re-opened. On several occasions, the security team had to escort them from the park. One even brought a megaphone and shouted obscenities at guests; apparently the children who came to gaze in wonder upon the ocean's mightiest carnivore were the reason the world was so terrible.

As rage grew over SeaLand's perceived mistreatment of Brody, forum threads over the "problem" grew and grew. Eventually it caught the eye of Heather and Sebastian, and they set their plan in action.

A very bad plan.

"We didn't really think it through as much as we should have," Heather Morton told me, which was the understatement of the century. The plan was to break into SeaLand well after midnight and dump a sack of rubber lacrosse balls into Brody's pool. Because Heather and Sebastian Morton apparently gathered all their intel from *Finding Nemo*, they failed to realize that the industrial-sized propellers in the industrial-sized filtration units designed to filter water in a 300,000 gallon pool would've crushed the lacrosse balls like one might squeeze the fragile head of a dandelion. They may have not even been noticed.

Regardless, they went about setting their plan into action. According to court documents, Heather Morton testified that they had donned black clothing and a backpack and parked at a local hotel adjacent to the marine park. "We knew we were probably going to jail that night," Heather Morton said. "We knew there's no way we could have snuck in, done what we were going to do, and escape without getting caught. To be honest...I think we wanted to get caught."

Of course they did. Many so-called activists live by the motto of "What good is an unseen deed?" This is especially true in the internet age, where people will frequently post selfies of themselves handing food to homeless, or incessantly blog about the volunteer work they're doing. Not to devalue the good these so-called "humble-braggers" do, but I prefer to live by a different motto: "When you do things right, people won't be sure you've done anything at all." (*Futurama,* "Godfellas," 2002). There are some that live by the creed that a good deed is its own reward, and others who prefer the adoration that deed brings.

"How else would anyone know it was us?" Heather Morton said, confirming my suspicions. "It was pretty easy to sneak in. We found a low fence that was covered by some bushes and overhanging trees. It was windy. Would've been hard to see us."

SeaLand of Myrtle Beach was not a facility prepared to handle an actual break-in. As James Warren explained to me later, "We have the typical problems of any zoo or amusement park. Drunk or high teenagers roaming around with their friends on a Saturday night with nothing else to do. We had enough security to handle them. They were always timid and easy to catch. It still wasn't a huge issue.

Maybe once or twice a year. We have five night guards that roam the park. We never really thought we needed any more. I mean, who breaks into a zoo? What are you going to steal? Are you going to haul a tiger out of there and keep it in your house? Are you going to put a shark in a fish bowl? We never really thought too much of it, to be completely honest."

Regardless, Sebastian and Heather Morton infiltrated SeaLand of Myrtle beach and headed into the Domain of the King. They had made their way onto the work island and dumped the lacrosse balls into the pool. Their plan, of course, was doomed from the start. Not only because the massive propellers in Brody's filters could crush lacrosse balls, but because lacrosse balls *sank*. Yes, they're made of rubber, but are also very heavy and dense. I learned this while coaching amateur lacrosse shortly after I graduated high school; one of the lacrosse balls hit my wrist during practice and shattered my expensive watch. By the next morning, all of the lacrosse balls were sitting on the bottom of Brody's pool, buried in the sand.

After dumping the lacrosse balls into the pool, the rebellious couple took some time to spray some graffiti on the stage. Neither were particularly good artists, so what was said is somewhat illegible even in the photographs, but what's important is that at one point, Sebastian Morton got down on his haunches near the edge of the work island in an attempt to coax Brody to the surface.

"I don't know what he was doing," Heather Morton told me at the diner. "I...I think he wanted to pet him or something. I honestly don't know."

Many animal rights activists have a slightly misshapen

view of animals and their behavior. We see similar beliefs, though to a lesser degree, with many dog owners. Despite what many want to believe, most animals, particularly the more primitive ones such as sharks and many reptiles, operate on instinct; the in-bred behavior that is embedded within their genetic code. It is not uncommon for people to confuse instinct with intuition; this is not accurate. Intuition is synonymous with a "hunch" based off experience, whereas instinct refers to behaviors an organism is born with and not necessarily learned over time.

The reality is that most animals have but one purpose: to survive. This is what drives them. Simple-minded animals, such as sharks, are driven by this sole goal to an even greater degree than others. The shark doesn't have empathy, it doesn't have sympathy.

This is what cost Sebastian Morton his life.

"It wasn't a f-cking puppy," Heather Morton recalled tearfully. "I guess he thought he had this connection with it, that he was helping its species or something so it would be grateful."

Brody wasn't.

Sebastian Morton patted the water in an attempt to get a good, up close look at Brody and the massive shark gave him much more than he had bargained for. The Great White shark opened its jaws wide and grabbed Sebastian by the arm. The shark then clamped down and yanked the young activist off the work island and into the water. He wouldn't let go.

"I panicked," Heather Morton said, her fingers rapping on her coffee cup. "I saw him get pulled into the water. It all just happened so fast. One second he was there, the next he was gone. I didn't know what to do. I saw blood. Lots and lots of blood."

I could tell that she was on the verge of throwing up. I had watched the tapes. I couldn't imagine going through what she had. Not seconds after Sebastian was dragged under, the water was bubbling with blood. The black silhouette that was Brody's enormous body thrashed in the water, beneath the moonlight. The blood appeared black in the nightlights, which themselves turned the water a shade of pale green. Chunks of flesh floated to the surface, as well as pieces of fabric and clumps of hair as Brody ripped the young man's body to shreds.

The security team arrived within minutes. They found a crying Heather Morton, looking down into the pool in hysterics. The love of her life had just been made into a meal by the very thing he was trying to save. That's a reality that still obviously haunts her to this day, as well as anyone who has seen the CCTV footage of that fateful night.

Brody had taken a human life. There was no getting around it. The pride of Myrtle Beach, who'd masked himself as a monster, now officially was.

13
Return to Sender

What happened set off a national debate on the safety of marine parks within hours of the news breaking. Suddenly, social media was abuzz and everyone had a different opinion. What had been a very rare and tragic incident had suddenly become an "epidemic" in the eyes of the public, as such things are wont to do. However, though rare, it wasn't exactly an unprecedented incident. As addressed earlier in this work, deaths at zoos had occurred before, many of which happened at marine parks. The killer whale that had killed Dawn Brancheau had been responsible for numerous deaths on its own.

"It was a mess," recalled Anna Harding. "I got a call in the middle of the night and headed down to the park right away. There were already ambulance crews, police, and even a few news vans on the scene. I don't know how those people got there before I did." She sighed. "There was a lot of blood. This is going to sound cold, but I was actually worried about how it might affect the water chemistry and harm Brody."

While SeaLand employees distracted the shark, what was left of Sebastian Morton was pulled from the water. His body had been decimated beyond recognition. Heather Morton had been detained at the police station a few miles away for questions and potential prosecuting. She would later serve three months for breaking and entering, with the death of Sebastian Morton being deemed an accident. Naturally, animal rights groups immortalized the young man and used the incident as another example of why Great Whites shouldn't be housed.

They got what they wanted after all.

"We were getting ready for a complete storm," James Warren told me. "After the [Dawn] Brancheau accident, SeaWorld was never the same. Hell, even guests were suing." He wasn't exaggerating. In the wake of the Brancheau incident, one family attempted to sue SeaWorld for emotional damages. They claimed their son had been traumatized by seeing the whale drag the trainer around. While this may have been true, it wasn't exactly SeaWorld's fault. Nevertheless, OSHA levied sanctions of $75,000 against the park. (A small sum, in my own opinion).

"A lot of people weren't fans of the pretty tiny fine SeaWorld got, but the reality is that they weren't *too* at fault," James Warren said. "They followed all the safety regulations. Trainers weren't even allowed in the water. Dawn Brancheau was killed when the whale forcibly thrust itself up onto the work island and grabbed her. There really wasn't a whole lot anyone could do about it."

I'm not certain that was true. Regardless, it was a work accident. An industrial accident. As distant as calling that seems.

"But over the next few days, I started to think that this would be more similar to the Daniel Dukes case."

In 1999, 27-year-old homeless man Daniel Dukes broke into SeaWorld of Orlando after closing, in a matter very similar to Sebastian and Heather Morton. What happened that night remains a mystery. All that's known is that his dead body was found in the tank of the killer whale Tilikum—yes, *that* same Tilikum—the next morning.

The accident was deemed just that: an accident. No footage of what occurred exists and the cause of death was determined to be drowning. Initial reports stated that Daniel Dukes was under the influence, but no alcohol nor drugs were found in his system.

Nothing significant came of the incident. Mostly because the victim had broken in and put himself in harm's way.

"Almost the exact same thing happened with us," said James Warren.

The investigation determined that Sebastian Morton had (obviously) broken into SeaLand illegally. OSHA performed a full check of the facilities and found that SeaLand of Myrtle Beach had absolutely no safety violations. Even the thin security team was found to be adequate. "I mean, this isn't the case of someone falling over a railing, here. This is a case of people knowingly breaking into our park and literally throwing themselves in a shark tank. We can't be held accountable for the stupidity of others." There were no lawsuits, which immediately prompted "Justice For Sebastian" tags to pop up all over the internet. After a few months, Warren and SeaLand hoped that everything would just sort of go away.

Brody's exhibit reopened several weeks later to almost no fanfare. The negative PR from the SeaLand Incident had irreparably damaged the exhibit.

James Warren recalled, "We had some thrill seekers, obviously. But most people now avoided the Domain of the

King, especially people with children. No one wanted to risk their kid seeing the shark rip apart another person, even though the odds of that happening again were somewhere around nil. Our merchandise was a big part of our profit pie, but without kids buying Brody t-shirts and plushies, we lost a ton of income. Not to mention that we were branded some evil organization on the internet. Even though there was literally nothing we could do to prevent that young man's death, people avoided us like we pulled the trigger."

Suddenly, the park that had become so profitable thanks to its star attraction was now suffering from it. Anna Harding, James Warren, and a number of other executives held a late night meeting to discuss the future, and on November 1, 2015, after several months in captivity, it was decided that it was time to return Brody to the ocean.

The announcement was met with acclaim from animal rights activists all over the planet. There was even a temporary spike in attendance as people wanted one more chance to get a good look at the king of the ocean. Alas, the decision had been made to send Brody home.

"Returning an animal like Brody to the sea is a process almost as complex as getting him into captivity in the first place," Anna Harding explained. "The first step was tagging. We tagged Brody with a tracking device so we could keep tabs on him and use his migration patterns for research once he was back in the wild. "And we couldn't just let him go on the coastline. Sure, let's go ahead and let a sixteen-foot shark loose on a popular beach swarming with tasty people."

SeaLand had gone through similar procedures for transporting Brody back to the water as they had for bringing him in. However, because there wasn't such a strict deadline this time, they were able to wait until midnight when there'd be no traffic.

"We brought in the crane and lifted Brody into a truck bed loaded with seawater. He wasn't happy," remembered Anna Harding. "Once we got to the marina, there was a barge waiting for us, also loaded with seawater." Brody was lifted into the barge and carried out to sea. "We got about twelve miles off the coast when we opened the back of the container and let Brody slip out into the water."

"You didn't have to acclimate him?" I asked.

"No, not in this case. The reason we had to acclimate him to the water in his pool was because that was an artificial environment. This was the sea. Natural. It was really anticlimactic, actually. He slipped into the water and just…vanished. The last memory I have of him is of the end of his tail slipping beneath the blackness. Then, he was gone. I wasn't worried, though. He'd be fine."

And he was fine. Anna pulled up her laptop during our interview and showed me the OCEARCH Global Shark Tracker. Here, every tagged shark in the world can be tracked. You can see their historical migratory patterns, where they stopped, even pictures with a little profile.

Anna pointed out Brody's trail. "The data we'll get from tracking Brody will be invaluable. Not to mention the lessons we learned from trying to keep him. He spends most of his time around South Africa, but if he ever happens to come by here again, I'll be sure to head out on a boat and pay the old guy a visit."

And so we returned to my original question: "Do you really think this was a good idea? Keeping a shark like that in captivity? In hindsight, anyway."

"That's a difficult answer," she said. "People see what they want to see. They see the world in black and white, right and wrong. It's hard, on the surface, to call what we did 'right,' and I understand that entirely. We're going to learn a lot about Great Whites from this tracking data, perhaps even enough to save some of them. Not to mention all the donations we received and awareness we raised. More than a few kids who came to see Brody are going to grow up wanting to be marine biologists now. There is no right answer here. Obviously, one person died, and another was scarred for life, so it's hard to weigh those things against the knowledge we'll have and the lessons we've learned. So, do I think it was a good idea? I do. Unfortunately, it didn't work out quite as well as we wanted it to. And that's all there is to say about it."

SeaLand of Myrtle Beach is currently in decline. It's not expected to last more than a couple more fiscal years. This pattern is consistent with the state of marine and zoological parks in general. The SeaLand Incident and the events leading up to it perfectly encapsulate the complex saga faced by modern zoos.

Mountain gorilla, south China tiger, Sumatran elephant, orangutan, western lowland gorilla, bonobo, chimpanzee, giant panda, loggerhead turtle, Yangtze porpoise, African wild dog, black-footed ferret, Indian elephant, snow leopard, dugong, giant tortoise, marine iguana, Lorde Howe stick insect, black softshell turtle, Hawaiian crow, axolotl, oryx, fringe-limbed tree frog, Chinese alligator, paddlefish, sturgeon, golden mole, all species of echidna, 26 species of lemur, Philippine crocodile, radiated tortoise...

These are some of the 4,574 species the International Union for Conservation of Nature and Natural Resources recognizes as critically endangered and would probably be extinct if not for the conservation efforts funded by zoos and aquariums.

While it's easy to criticize zoos who fail to keep their animals healthy and safe—and there are many, as undoubtedly all apples contain a few bad seeds—behind the comfort of a keyboard, it is impossible to understate the importance of their role in raising awareness for endangered creatures and fighting for their protection.

Say what you want regarding zoos based on reading half of a biased headline and false stereotypes, but there is one fact that is inescapable even for the most bitter internet mob: if not for the wildlife programs paid for by the cost of your admission, many of your favorite animals would not exist. If zoos suddenly disappeared, so would most of the species you see in them.

Currently, the Great White shark is currently listed as a threatened species by the IUCN. While the costs were grim, it is the hope of many that thanks to the awareness raised by the efforts of SeaLand of Myrtle Beach—and the unfortunate tragedies surrounding it—that one day, their numbers will rise, and the king of the oceans will no longer be in danger of vanishing into memory.

BRENT ANDREW SALTZMAN was born on July 29, 1988 near Washington DC. He graduated from Radford University in 2011.

Lightning Source UK Ltd.
Milton Keynes UK
UKHW011836050619
343933UK00001B/7/P